KRISHNAMURTI

FOR BEGINNERS™

BY JUAN CARLOS KREIMER

ILLUSTRATED BY MÁRTIN ARVALLO

Writers and Readers Publishing, Inc.
P.O. Box 461, Village Station
New York, NY 10014

Writers and Readers Limited
35 Britannia Row
London N1 8QH
Tel: 0171 226 3377
Fax: 0171 359 1454
e-mail: begin@writersandreaders.com

Spanish Edition:
Krishnamurti para Principiantes,
published by ERA NACIENTE SLR
Arce 287
Buenos Aires (1426)
Argentina

Translated by Latin Words - Stephanie D'Oray_ Caroline Maldonado
Book design by Emma Byrne

A Writers and Readers Documentary Comic Book
Copyright © 1998
ISBN # 0-86316-276-2 Trade
1 2 3 4 5 6 7 8 9 0

Printed in Finland by WSOY

Contents

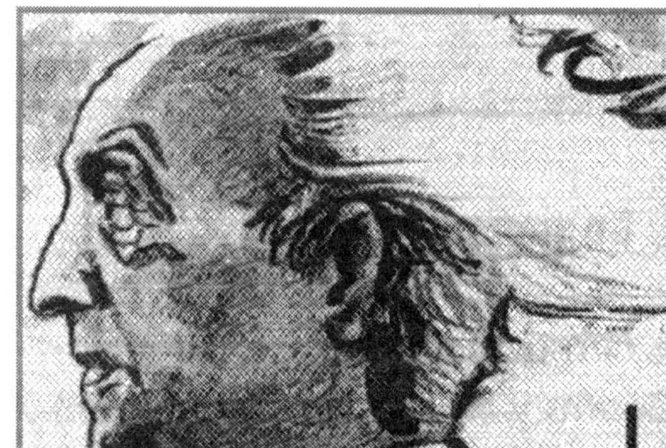

Krishnamurti

(1895-1986) was not intending to promote ideas about truth: he was developing and expressing ideas about the nature of the mind which searches for truth - its conditioning, and the tricks it plays on itself. Listening to his vibrant and magnetic talks, his audience could not fail to take on a special state of awareness, which he claimed, was the essence of knowledge itself.

Yes. The more that **K** rejected his role as a teacher, the more he taught. For millions of men and women who attended his lectures, or who read him in any of the 47 languages into which his books were translated, his ideas were, and continue to be, synonymous with **inner psychological and spiritual liberation.**

20 years before K was born..

1. The Messiah

New York, 1875. New York circles linked to the esoteric tradition were focussed around **Madame Helena Petrovna Blavatsky** (also known as **HPB**), a young Russian emigrée. Impressed by her clairvoyance and other skills as a medium, they used to believe that through her they could hear the voices of the Masters of the Occult Brotherhood.

Together with Colonel Henry Steel Olcott, a lawyer and American government official, who wrote about psychic phenomena and spiritual apparitions, and William Q. Judge, another lawyer, **Mrs Blavatsky** decided to set up an international organisation. According to her, the Masters Koot Humi (or Kuthumi), Lal Singh and Morya were the true founders of the **Theosophical Society** . The name has Greek roots: **Theo** = *God*; **Sophia** = Wisdom.

1. Anyone can acquire knowledge of the transcendental reality by means of divine communication and practice of the occult tradition.

2.. All religions are born of the same root of eternal wisdom, of myths and symbols which repeat themselves throughout the centuries.

3... The study of these secrets will lead to the truth and spiritual unity.

India, 1879. HPB and Olcott decided to merge the TS with an Indian movement which recognised "The return of the Vedas" (sacred books). In Bombay, Mrs Blavatsky began to receive periodic communications from Master K.H. The messages that fell onto the page appeared to be dictated letters. There were those who said that she had written the letters herself. The British Museum has preserved more than a hundred of these letters.

Thanks to **The Theosophist**, a magazine published by Mrs Blavatsky and Olcott and which became popular among English colonials living in India and high-caste Indians, Theosophy had begun to be well known in several European countries. In the old summer house in Adyar, near Madras, to where the head office of the magazine moved in 1982 - and where, even today the Theosphical Society continues to function - Mrs Blavatsky spent long periods shut up in a temple that she had built so that so that the Masters could communicate with her.

1885. While HPB and Olcott travelled throughout Europe, a couple who looked after her house made known the existence of letters written by HPB in which certain tricks were revealed. An investigator from the Society for Psychical Research in London, made a special journey to inspect the place. He published a report saying that HPB's letters were fraudulent.

We will never know if HPB's housekeepers wanted to ruin her reputation. Neither if the informant had seen only what he wanted to see and ignored all other evidence. Even though her detractors said she was 'interpreting' the ancient Book of Dyzan, for her the important thing was to put into words the thoughts that the Mahatmas had imprinted upon her mind...

EVOLUTION
In relation to the Universe (cosmogenesis)and with humanity (anthropogenesis)

1. The ultimate reality as an all powerful and transcendental principal beyond the reach of thought.
2. Universality of the Law of Cycles through the medium of nature.
3. The identification of all souls into the Universal Soul and its pilgrimage across the most diverse conditions of intelligence. by means of re-incarnation. in accordance with the Law of Cycles and Karma.

London 1889. **Annie Wood Besant** (also known as **AB**), an ardent free thinker and campaigner of women's rights, trade unionism, Fabian socialism etc unexpectedly joined the Theosophical Society. She had read "**The Secret Doctrine**", the book just published by Mrs Blavatsky, and was deeply moved by it.

***HPB** brought to light the existence of the Occult Hierarchy, made up of the Masters of Wisdom, visible and invisible, who look after and guide the world, preserving the most ancient knowledge of the profound Laws of Life and the Universe.*

In 1891 HPB died and Annie Besant began to run the Esoteric Section of the Theosophical Society with the American lawyer Judge. But they fell out permanently over its control and in 1895 Judge created the Theosophical Society of America, which he dominated until his death the following year. A year later, the other founder, Olcott, died.

Annie Besant allied herself with the Church of England priest and clairvoyant **Charles Walter Leadbeater** (also known as **CWL**) who became the vice-secretary of the European Section of the Society. Between the two of them, they managed to increase the numbers of members enormously.

Back in India, 1893. Annie Besant moved to India and thus began her passionate attachment to this cause, which would last for the rest of her life. Many young intellectuals, influenced by her passion, joined the Theosphical Society - one of whom was **Jawaharlal Nehru.** Annie Besant continued to campaign for social and political reform, as President of the Indian Congress Party.

India 1895.

The **Jiddu** family was living in Madnapalle, a village in the south. **Naraniah,** the father, was an orthodox Brahmin, who worked for the British Administration; he was also a Theosophist. **Sanjeevana,** his wife, was a very religious, and a devotee of **Krishna,** the shepherd God. She had paranormal powers and she could make predictions.

Sanjeevana was not disturbed by breaking laws with the tradition which maintained that the puja, the room for meditation, could be entered only after taking a ritual bath and putting on clean clothes. The room could never be used as a resting place for the dying, nor for giving birth and never be used by a woman during menstruation. But it was there, at 12.30 on the 12th of May, that the eighth son of the Jiddu family came into the world, and so his mother showed that her intuition had been right.

The following day, and astrologer predicts:

Contrary to the prophecies, **Krishnamurti** (**K** from here on), was a weak and sickly child. He had frequent nosebleeds, and experienced a dramatic attack of malaria when he was two years old. He was not in the least interested in school or in studying. Because of his indistinct way of speaking, limited vocabulary and a lost expression, his teachers thought he was somewhat backward.

Neither his teachers or any other adults noticed his highly developed capacity of observation. (which would be a characteristic of his throughout his entire life), nor his extreme generosity. His brother, **Nityananda** (Nitya, also known as **N**) who was born three years later, and showed more vitality, character and intelligence, naturally took on the mission of looking after him and bring him back to earth when K could not escape from his dreams.

1901. K is initiated as a **Brahmin**. For Hindus, the Brahmachaya is the first step in the life of a Brahmin.

Besides passing many hours a day very close to his mother, he shared with her a special gift; he could see clearly people who had recently died. **K** was nine years old when his older sister died: he and Sajeevana would see her walking in the garden during the following months.

A year and a half later, when his mother died suddenly, **K** shifted between moments of confusion with visions of his mother carrying out her daily tasks. **K** showed great interest in all kinds of mechanical things.

Adyar, 1908. The Jiddu family - father and four sons between 5 and 15 - arrived in the city where the Theosophical Society had its headquarters. Narianah had had to retire one year before. He managed, through writing several letters to Annie Besant, to obtain a job as secretary of the Esoteric Section. They offered him a very simple small house, without a bath. **K** and his brother **N** had to walk nearly ten kilometres every day to attend a local school.

A few weeks later, Leadbeater also arrived. When Annie Besant was chosen as president in 1907, she confirmed Narianah's employment, and although he was given no official post, he was entrusted with all the correspondence that arrived in India from all parts of the world. A Dutch secretary, Johan van Maren, accompanied Leadbeater and an English short hand typist, Ernest Wood. In the evening, after finishing work, the three men would go swimming in the river.

In the first half of the 20th Century, the **British Governors of India** regarded Indians as an necessary part of the landscape. They had to be kept at a certain distance; in the best of cases they could be tolerated, but familiarity shouldn't be encouraged. An attitude of superior condescension dominated relations. It was within this atmosphere that the young Krishna was recognised, in a flash of psychic perception, by an eccentric British mystic.

Leadbeater asked **K**'s father to let him go to college, as he intended to take over his education. Narianah agreed on condition that his other son also got the same advantages. Leadbeater told Annie Besant about his 'discovery'.

Four tutors took on **K**'s and his brother's physical development. They taught them English and other subjects, made them take up sport, provided healthy food for them, told them to grow their hair (It was shaved high on the forehead) and gave them clean clothes every morning.

Tired of always telling him the same thing, one day **CWL** slapped him on the chin. **K** finally closed his mouth. From then on, although they spent some important moments together, **K** never felt the same about the man who was in charge of the **occult education** of the new Messiah.

Buddha, Mohammed, Christ, Moses, Lord Krishna... According to Hindu legends, they are reincarnated to save humanity. The expectations of Judeo- christianity of the coming of a new Messiah are refueled by numerous sayings of Esoteric Buddhism. Astride both faiths, the young **K** begins to be considered the reincarnation of the Lord Maitreya, the Bodhisattva of loving kindness.

In the beginning of the 20th century, and especially since the beginning of the spread of **Freud**'s theories about the unconscious, any signs of mysticism (not only Messianic) was considered to be psychopathological. The paradox was, that if there was one message that was held in common by most of the spiritual movements that arose at the end of this century, including the Judeo-Christian religions, it was this: "God is in you", or "You are your own Messiah".

Did the boy **K** understand what is happening around him? Later on, when he was questioned about these first meetings, he just answered "*I don't remember*".
In any case, he already seemed to know that there was something 'special' in him. Although there were things he didn't understand, he believed in this strength, in the presence of "an Other", more than in the "environment' created around him. Given who he was, and seeing beyond the tests that were being planned for him, **K** knew that he was here on earth to obey this voice.

During several months, every night, Leadbeater took him, "in his astral form", before Master Kuthumi for fifteen minutes instruction. In the mornings **K** struggled to write down the phrases he remembered.

These notes combined the theosophic teaching with certain basic principles of Buddhism. Leadbeater edited them immediately and published them as a book called "*At the Feet of the Master*". They were translated into 27 languages over the following years. Although **Alcyone** is though to be the author, readers from all over the world sent letters to the Theosphical Society, thanking **K** for having written it. The readers said that his words had changed their lives.

Ernest Wood and Leadbeater drew up an agreement to be signed by **K**'s father.

At the end of 1908, on arriving from a trip to the USA and Europe, during which she had been talking of the imminent arrival of the World Teacher, Annie Besant saw the brothers for the first time in Madras railway station. In the headquarters of the Theosophical Society in Adyar, she closely followed the education of both of them. One day, she decided to make the situation official.

Doesn't he deserve to be let in?
Yes.
The Master smiles on them.
1910.
During days and nights, Leadbeater and K remained closed in the rooms allotted to Annie Besant, who had gone to a conference in Benares. Leadbeater and K received instructions from the astral plane. They left their own bodies, travelled far away; they only returned occasionally in order to eat.
?

A magazine **The Herald of the Star**, was also established, in Adyar 25,000 copies were printed only for subscribers. The magazine had offices in 50 countries.

Daily News
I feel an everlasting reverence for Buddha.
Where one sees the little Star of the Planet shining, one knows that the heart beneath it beats with hope and happiness. All the members of the Society who believed in the Advent had to wear the Silver Star, so as not to find themselves left behind in the world, less alert than those who were not theosophists.
Next week. will Krishnamurti be in London? Yes!

London. As soon as she arrived at Charing Cross Station with the 'brothers', Annie Besant started to be severely attacked by old friends and admirers. They accused her of having made the Messiah into a business.

Rudolf Steiner, an eminent German Theosophist. split with the Theosophical Society and started his own movement, the **Anthroposophy** 'Spiritual Science',which developed unique methods of education, medicine, agriculture and diverse artistic expressions with innovative characteristics.

Lady Emily Lutyens (wife of Edwin Lutyens, the architect who designed New Delhi) , was one of the first English women to join the Order of the Star of the East. Other distinguished women offered **K** and Nitya their homes, taking them for trips in the country in deluxe cars, and to the theatre...

On return to India. Every time the train stopped, a large crowd gathered alongside K's carriage, calling for him to come out. K discovered a safe refuge: he shut himself in the toilet.

On arrival, they found that the number of members had continued to increase despite the number of criticisms. Leadbeater had organised an enormous meeting in Benares. At this conference, somebody suggested accrediting the members by giving them certificates. More than 400 people - high-caste Indians British officials, victorian ladies, old people and children, were seated close together on the ground, waiting for their diplomas. Each time that **K** handed one out, it was as if the spirit were descending. Members of the Order couldn't resist prostrating themselves in front of **Krishna**.

...there were not enough diplomas to go round.

Adyar, 1912.

Influenced by orthodox Hindus, who were opponents of Theosophy, and by anti-British extremists, Narianah announced in a letter to Annie Besant that he would take her to court unless she gave him back custody of his sons.

Their father seemed to calm down. However, when **K** and Nitya left for Bombay several days earlier than planned, and Annie Besant ordered that Narianah be expelled from the Theosophical Society, he started the legal battle.

In fact, the brothers did not return to India until 1921. To start with, they lived in a large house in Ashdown Forest, in Sussex, lent to them by Lady de Warr. Two disciples of Leadbeater were their tutors. They lived in great luxury; they went to smart parties, were waited upon by servants, and learnt to play tennis. They dressed very well. However, what fascinated **K** most was a Harley Davidson motor bike. He took it apart and re-assembled it several times.

After two judgements, which ordered her to return the boys to their father, Annie Besant appealed to the Privy Council and won the case, due to the fact that neither K nor Nitya wanted to go back to Adyar to testify.

K showed little sign of complying with the obligations imposed on him. Some members of the Theosophical Society commented that he had lost interest in esoteric activities. Had he become a sceptic? Was he beginning to leave his spiritual destiny behind him?

During these years of separation, the correspondence between Annie Besant and **K** continued on a regular basis. She did not lose interest in him, and he always showed his gratitude to his mentor.

1914. At the outbreak of the First World War, K and Nitya offered their services to the crown. In vain: racial prejudice was at its height. The brothers felt very alone, unhappy and totally rebuffed. Their intention of getting admission to an Oxford or Cambridge college collapsed. K was incapable of passing the entrance exams.

When they tried to get into the University, only Nitya got through the exam. *"At this time, K was only really interested in poetry... he loved Keats and Shelley,"* Lady Emily remembered. Together with George Arndale, she edited the extended international edition of the magazine *"The Herald of the Star"*.

France 1918. Leadbeater was away in Australia, Annie Besant was more interested in the independence of India than the coming of the Messiah, Nitya was studying law in London and Lady Emily was looking after her five children.

K thought that it was high time to take command of his own affairs. He traveled to Paris and stayed with his friends, the Manziarly family, who introduced him to the Paris life. He met dancers, writers, painters, and musicians. A new, fascinating and creative world was opened up to him.

Annie Besant had returned to London and asked him to accompany her to Theosophical Society events, and to oversee the publication of the Star.

K felt a conflicting reaction to the visit to London of **Rajagopal**, another past disciple of Leadbeater. Rajagopal was thought, at the age of twenty, to have been Saint Bernard in another life. On one hand, he was happy that the Theosophical Society was becoming stronger again, but on the other that it might start to admire him again too much. Sitting in a cheap hotel room, suffering from a cold, K writes:

In Paris, **K** not only learnt to speak good French. He also started to give talks to the Theosophical Society of his own volition and the simple desire to be useful. He wanted to return to India.

Adyar, 1921. After nine years of absence, K and Nitya returned to India. *"A new chapter"* said Annie Besant when she welcomed them. During this visit, K made new friends, took note of the atmosphere around him and re-established contact with the Masters. (Spiritual beings who according to belief, were living within superior people in Tibet). He wrote to Lady Emily:

Paris. Bad news: In May it is discovered that Nitya has a patch on his lung. **K** wanted him to be treated by a French naturopath. The brothers stayed in a house just outside Paris.

Paris. Good news: In July, Annie Besant arrives for an enormous Theosophical Convention. More than by his impeccable French **K** displays in the inauguration, the 2,000 members are impressed by his understanding of the problems put forward and his grasp and handling of the debate. Once the Convention was over, he concentrated on looking after Nitya.

Amsterdam. On the way to meet a dutch Baron, Van Pallandt, who wants to leave him an eighteenth century castle in Eerde with 200 hectares of land, **K** spent some time in Amsterdam. He met a seventeen year old American girl, Helen Knothe, the niece of a Dutch Theosophist, and, for the first time in his life, fell in love.

Adyar. Believing that Nitya was better, **K** planned another trip to India with his brother, Annie Besant had built a room for them onto a house in the headquarters of the Theosophical Society; from their balcony the river Adyar could be seen running into the sea. In a talk, **K** predicted the future when he stated: *"He [the next Teacher] is not going to preach what we want...but on the contrary He is going to wake us all up whether we like it or not..."*

Australia, 1922. K and Nitya arrived in Sidney for a Theosophical Society Conference. His old tutor, Leadbeater, had just been appointed archbishop of the Liberal Catholic Church, an ancient Jansenist sect, which claimed descent from the apostles. Dressed in a crimson soutane, and wearing a cross, he officiated at church services. Unwillingly, **K** attended one of these out of politeness.

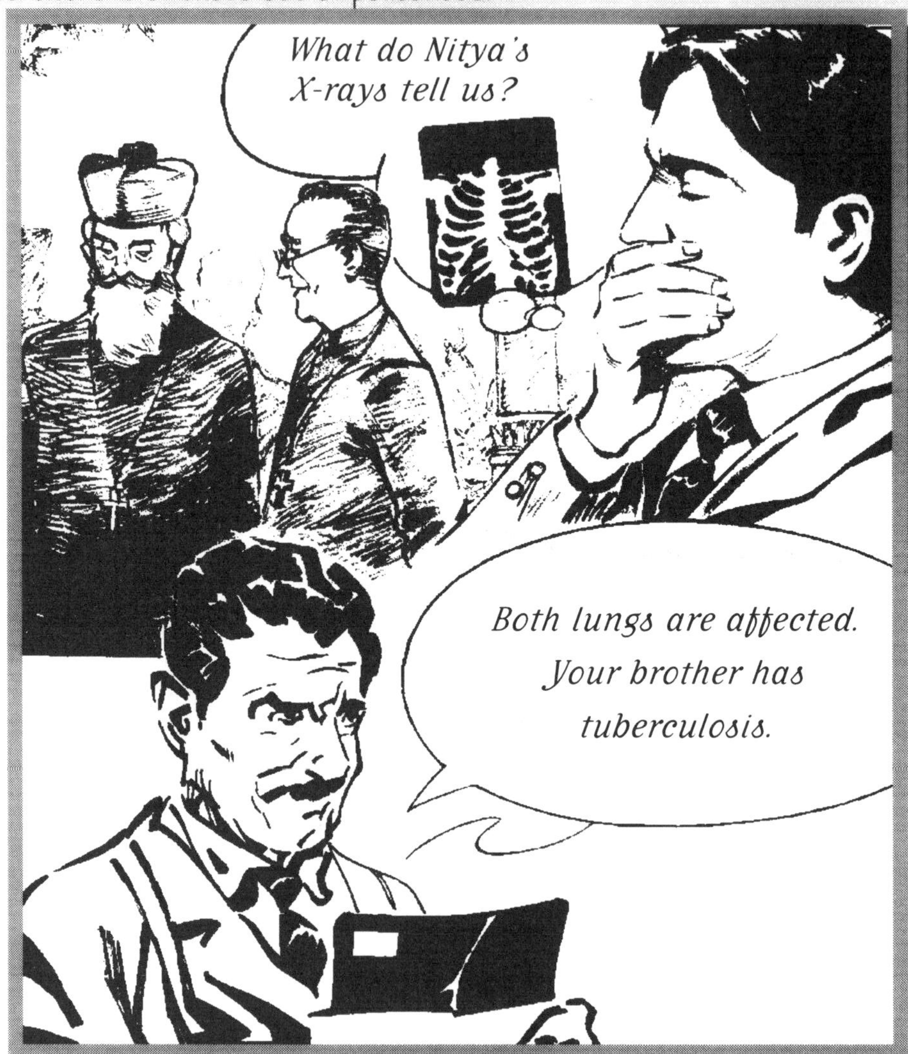

K and Nitya have to return urgently to Switzerland. They travel via San Francisco, to visit **Ojai,** a valley near Santa Barbara and visit a cabin that Mrs Gray, an American Theosophist, offers them. The climate of this part of California is ideal for the cure of tuberculosis, she tells them. During his lifetime, **K** returns to Ojai frequently - he also died here, in 1986.

II. Spiritual Awakening

Ojai, 1922.

Enchanted with the beauty of the countryside and the grandeur of the californian redwoods, which looked like enormous cathedrals, **K** and Nitya enjoyed some privacy for the first time in their lives. In another house nearby lived Mr Warrington, a Theosophist; the vicar of the Liberal Catholic Church and a friend of the daughter of Mrs Gray, Rosalind Williamson. This nineteen year old girl developed an affectionate and caring relationship with Nitya.

* K was referring to Helen Knoth

Without the problems of class, caste or race which he encountered in India and England, nor the pressures due to being the Messiah, **K** started to meditate regularly every morning and spent the rest of the day doing whatever he felt like. He read O'Henry and the New Testament. His only worries were the prevailing heat and the health of his brother.

In the afternoon of Thursday 17th August, **K** felt tired and anxious. A discomfort which began as a contraction in the shoulders, turned into a very strong pain in the nape of the neck and the spine. When he touched his neck, he discovered a lump the size of a walnut. He slept well, but the next day after breakfast, he began to shake and moan as if something had wounded him inside.

Those who saw him come and go from those uncontrollable states that arose within him, supposed that **K** was being 'brought through' to the Masters and forces from another plane had taken over his body. He was irritated by anyone who brushed past his bed, raised their voice or made the floor creak, even the breeze coming in through the blinds. When he was in pain he called for silence, peace and darkness. When he was calmer he reverted to speaking in his mothertongue, Telugu, as though he were in Adyar.

There was a man mending the road; that man was myself;
...the pickaxe he held was myself; the very stone which he was breaking up was a part of me; the tender blade of grass was my very being, and the tree beside the man was myself.
I was in everything, or rather everything was in me, inanimate and animate, the mountain, the worm, and all breathing things.

During the next three days, K continued to suffer terrible pains. He trembled, often fainted, entered and left semi-conscious states. With each new attack, he seemed to go further away. It was as if he had emptied out his consciousness, or as if he were before a Great Presence.

Sunday 20th August. It was getting late. The house was filled with an even more powerful force. **K** was possessed. He wanted nobody near him. That night, those watching him in the garden (Rosalind, the priest and the neighbour) knew that his body had been prepared for the Great One.

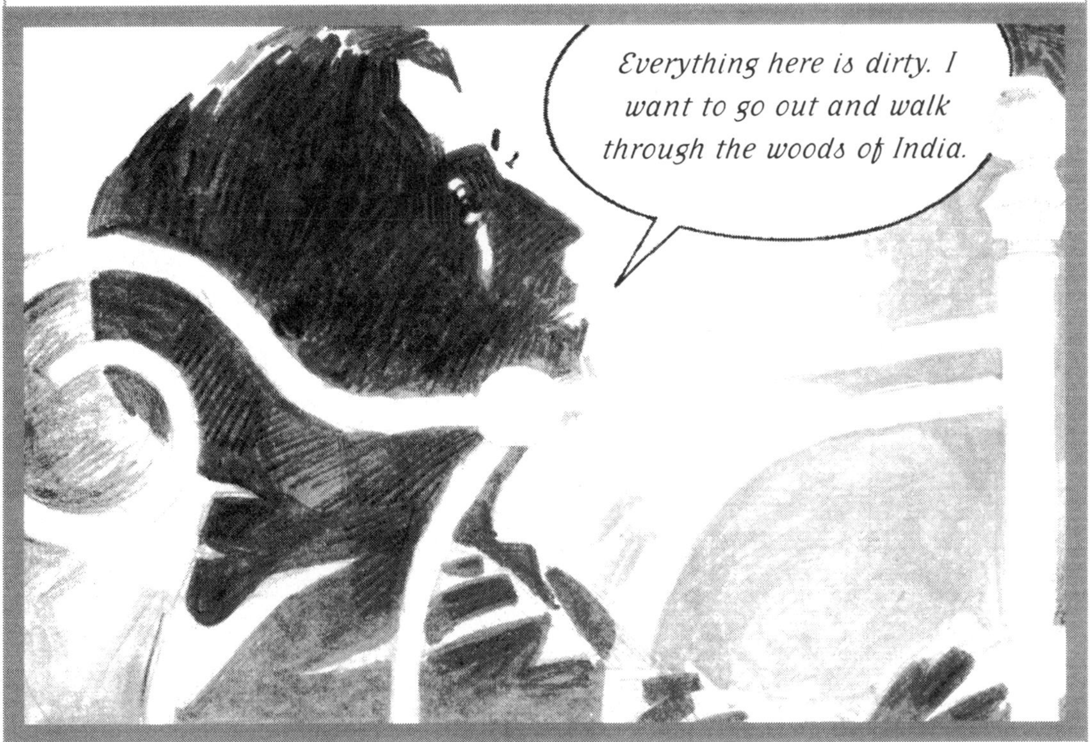

Everything here is dirty. I want to go out and walk through the woods of India.

Mr Warrington coaxed him to go out and sit under the pepper tree.

K spent the whole of Monday under the pepper tree. The trembling returned, but less frequently and with less intensity.

Silence grows and intensifies. It becomes more profound. The mind has paid attention to the landscape and now it is silent. It has done so naturally with no effort. It is as confident as a bird that spreads its wings. It has folded itself into itself so as to penetrate to whatever lies at greater depths. That is a dimension that the mind can not yet grasp or comprehend. Also there is no witness to the depth of it. Every part of the whole of one's being is alert and sensitive, but absolutely silent. That which is new, this profundity, is expanded, distanced. It renews itself its own bursting open, beyond time and space.

Nitya's description coincided with Hindu texts which referred to the Kundalini. This force would be energy in a free state. **K** said that this 'process, and others which he experienced in the following years, helped him to become the channel for some powerful force. This force would be the source of his future teachings.

1924. After the 'process', the attitude of **K** towards the Mission underwent a profound change. With revitalized energy, he undertook an enormous tour of numerous centres of Theosophy in the US, England and Austria. Those were months of incessant activity: conferences, meetings, conventions. In Arnhem (Holland), he presided over a Theosophical Congress attended by thousands. He wrote monthly for *The Herald*, answered letters, made acquaintance with personalities and artists. He lived on an annual allowance.

There is too much influence of the church here. Our work is in Ojai.

•Anyone who saw the group that keeps **K** company in the house he had been lent in the Tyrol thought that they were a group of people with no worries or obligations, typical of the roaring twenties.

•Anyone who saw **K** so happy and alive could never imagine the pains and the internal torture he had to suffer during the night.

Before returning to California, the group traveled to India and Australia. **K** visited his birthplace and decided to build a school nearby. It was established the year after in Rishi Valley, with money from the Trust, the first of eight he founded. In Sydney he realised that he and Leadbeater spoke different spiritual languages. Nitya's health was getting worse.

Ojai, 1925. While K was looking after his brother, strange news reached him from London, India and Sydney; those closest to him (including Annie Besant) were starting to assign themselves the roles of apostles. They stated that they had gone through various levels of initiation in the astral plane, transmitting instructions from the Masters. They tried to establish rules of co-existence between them and the non-initiated. They went to the extreme of wanting to wear silk underwear and sumptuous robes. Leadbeater approved. K remained sceptical: for him the Path of Enlightenment was something different.

During those nights, K had recurring dreams - he was before the Great Brotherhood and was asking about Nitya's health. He offered to sacrifice his happiness in exchange for his recovery. He was ready to do whatever was necessary to save the life of his brother. Leadbeater and Annie Besant wrote to him, telling him the same.

K feels relieved: he has faith in the Masters.

London. In October, when Annie Besant asks him to travel with her to India to celebrate the 50th anniversary of the Theosophical Society, the first thing he thought about was who would look after Nitya. As his brother seemed better and Madame de Manziarly came to look after him, K left at once for Europe. There he came into contact with the Twelve Apostles and perceived the power they assumed inside and outside the Theosophical Society.
This business of the apostles has a limit. Something so infinitely precious, sacred and private has been made publicly ugly and ridiculous, cheap and vulgar.
Why don't you speak to Annie Besant?
What good would that do? The apostles would say that dark forces have taken possession of me.

Naples. Before leaving for Colombo (capital of what was then Ceylon, now Sri Lanka) George Arundale and Wedgwood wanted **K** to give them recognition of their status.
Acknowledge that we are apostles!
If you want the life of Nitya to be spared, make it happen!
As if it were part of this set of pressures, two telegrams from Nitya were waiting at the port: "I have flu". "It's rather more serious. Pray for me". Immovable in his faith, **K** believed that Maitreya and Buddha would not have let him leave Ojai if his brother was going to die. He felt that this nightmare will soon be over.

In fact, three days later, on the 13th of November, while a storm was rocking the boat at the entrance to the Suez canal, another telegram announces **the death of Nitya**.

Adyar
K emerged serenely from his battle with sorrow, free from all sentiment or emotion. However, his belief in the Masters and the occult hierarchy had undergone a total change.
The Masters will be in Holland and want to see us all together. Let's go!

Holland, 1926. Delegates of the Theosophical Society from all over the world, plus three thousand disciples and journalists from international newspapers gathered in the **Ommen camp** with the expectation that something supernatural would happen. **K** arrived with Annie Besant and gave talks around the camp fires and stated that he had come to build, not to destroy. Many present noticed that his words contradicted the teaching of orthodox Theosophy. The leaders of the Theosophical Society were very disturbed.

Eerde Castle. In this same place, the ancestral home of Baron Phillip van Pallandt, given to the trust in 1921 - when **K** was 26 years old and she 17, he met Helen Knothe. She was a violin student who aroused a deep love in him, although it was not possessive. They wrote to each other very often.

* Amma: this was the familiar name that K gave to AB.

The following year, when Helen visited him in Ojai, his passion seemed to have been dissipated. A short time afterwards, she married an American environmentalist.

Ojai, 1927. Annie Besant and **K** spent some months together. When she saw him being so happy she decided to buy more land nearby and to open a school. Later this became the Happy Valley Foundation.

Hollywood. K delivered his first public lecture in the US, to an audience of 16,000 people, who, according to the Los Angeles Times, "listened to him intently". K spoke of *Happiness through Freedom.*

K also confessed:

- I have never read a theosophical book. I do not understand that jargon.
- I meditate automatically, because it is part of theosophic belief. But meditation doesn't have any meaning for me.
- When I say I am at one with the Beloved, it is only to wake in your hearts and minds the desire to search for the truth.
- Truth lives in every one of you.

Faced with this type of idea, the old Theosophical leaders began to be worried: if such ideas were to get around, what would happen to their authority? By whom would the followers be guided? How would his power grow?

Variety . **John Barrymore** offered **K** $5,000 a week to play the lead in a film about the life of Buddha. **K** realised that he could earn his own living if he needed to. **Cecil B. de Mille** also wanted to introduce him to the world of cinema.

Holland, 1928. K took part in the Ommen Camp. Several thousand people came together for 10 days. K reiterated explicitly that each person should live from their own interior light. Reactions were not slow in coming.

So ... you no longer think you are God?

Neither Buddha nor Christ ever affirmed their divinity. It was the disciples who through their love imposed divinity on the master.

Another thing: could you tell me what your golfing handicap is?

Yes. I have a handicap of two.

The philosopher Joseph Campbell compared this moment of K's life with that of Jesus when he said "I have not come to bring peace, but the sword," or when he threw the merchants out of the temple.

When the time of the camp was over, K was brimming with happiness. He felt at one with the universe. However, only those who knew him well understood that his new stand irritated the hierarchy of the Theosophical Society even more.

K warned in public that he would dissolve the Order of the Star if it aspired to be the sole guardian of the truth. Hundreds of people all over the world became anxious about the news.

Antonio Bourdelle (sculptor)

Adyar. When **K** arrived in India, Annie Besant had dissolved the Esoteric section of the Theosophical Society. She was concerned with various questions: the omnipotence of Maitreya, who had abandoned **K**, **K**'s future; and the disintegration of the Theosophical movement... everyone had a premonition that a rupture was coming closer. **K** was beginning to be considered a secular philosopher, hostile to all religious beliefs. He seemed more interested in buying some land north of Benares, on the banks of the Ganges, to set up another school.

While his followers read his poems, **K** shut himself in his room and read detective stories. One of his favorite authors was Edgar Wallace.

Ommen 1929. Since the First World War, Europe had asked itself: How can this have happened? How could we have avoided it? What has emerged from all this devastation? In this climate the arrival of a better and wiser being who knew all the answers, seemed to be a ray of sunshine which appeared after all the torment. But he who had been prepared over 18 years to guide humanity toward salvation, not only dissolved the Order, but also invalidated the coming of the World Teacher.

K told them:

The devil and a friend are walking down the road ... suddenly a man appears in front of them and picks up something from the road.

They observe that he puts something in his pocket.

The friend asks the devil. " What was it that he picked up"? The devil answers: he picked up a fragment of truth.

The friend: "That must be bad business for you "The devil:" Oh no. on the contrary. My business is to let the man organise it.

The truth cannot be organised

Over the next years several women around **K** got married, others followed their own way, others simply moved away. Few people from this intimate circle of followers accompanied him to the end. One of these was **Mar de Manziarly**.

Except for the area used as the camp, **K** gives back the castle at Eerde to Baron van Pallandt, the land given to him in Australia and other donations. At the end of that year, when he was travelling to Adyar with Annie Besant, he gave up the Theosophical Society too.

"There is nobody you can follow, except you yourself"

To state this in a year approaching 2,000 is not the same as in 1930. Today it is an idea that is accepted worldwide. At that time, it resulted in something more like cataclysm, rather than as a true revelation. Neither Lady Emily Lutyens, K's great fiend, who for the last twenty years had let herself tell him openly what others thought in private, warned him that it was a declaration of real psychological and spiritual independence. Almost a political gesture!

On abandoning dependence and developing a new model of independence or interdependence, the fear of solitude is always present. At the same time, if we are not alone, it is very difficult to answer one's own questions. It is no accident that **solitude** should have become one of **K's** central themes.

1930. From this year onwards, the annual camps in Ommen and Ojai were open to the public. It was a different class of audience: people came who were interested in what K had to say, not in who he was, or was not.

The donations for his work continued to flow. **Rajagopal**, his secretary and confidant, looked after all the financial affairs, managed his trips and besides this, took charge of the publication of his lectures. He was an excellent organiser.

Indubitably, **K** possessed the power to cure, but he always showed himself to be very reticent about using it. He didn't want anyone to turn to him as a physical healer. He had filed away the power of clairvoyance that he had had in his youth.

K practiced this healing on himself, questioning everything constantly, including his own thoughts and teachings. He didn't want to remember anything from the past, and wanted to rid himself of the weight of memory. He stayed for long periods 'alert in silence'.

Adyar, 1933. After travelling through India, in May, **K** saw Annie Besant for the last time. She died in September, and a few months later, Leadbeater died too. **K** did not stay in the house of the Theosophical Society, but on the other side of the river, in Vasanta Vihar, in a house specially built for him and his enterprise.

The car took them to Rishi Valley, where the co-educational school was being run, that is to say, where the teachers and the pupils learnt together.

Not only was it difficult to find teachers who agreed with these principles, but parents of the pupils found it difficult to agree that a 'good education' did not include entrance to a university. In India, then, as now, only a qualification lead to a good job.

Let go of your personality. patriotism. heroism. the competitive spirit. religious faith... they are all prejudices.

New Zealand. The New Zealand government forbid the transmission of K's talks, because they were considered controversial. **George Bernard Shaw**, a companion of Annie Besant's socialist beginnings, was also under attack, and jumped to his defence in the epilogue of his play ***Androcles and the Lion***..

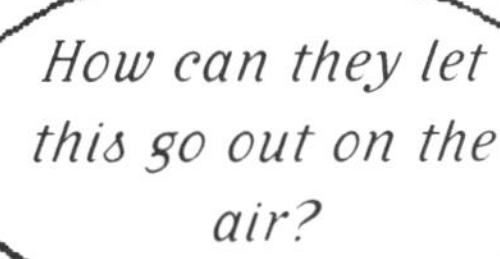

K was unconcerned that some strongly catholic countries considered him anti-religious. He wrote, talked and expressed what was in his mind, as surprised as someone who has had a revelation for the first time. He felt himself overcome by a mental state similar to those experienced by the writer of the ***Song of Songs,*** Buddha, Jesus...

Montevideo 1935...

In eight months of travelling around Latin America, K spoke at 25 conferences. Crowds of people came to hear him in Brazil, Uruguay, Argentina and Chile. In Buenos Aires, the catholic church organised a demonstration and handed out flyers criticising his ideas, especially the one stating : **"Transformation does not call for renunciation, but discernment."**

This authority undermines thought and the love of yourselves

get out !

get out !

get out !

In spite of the insults and threats to his security, K did not let it upset him. It was not because he was insensitive or thoughtless.

You applaud me too quickly because you yourselves have created these exploiters.

I have no image of myself. nor any ideology.

The image is resistance. When this does not exist. there is vulnerability but no psychological damage.

WE ARE AGAINST KRISHNAMURTI GET OUT!!!

get out !

the crowd shout the slogan
DEPORT KRISHNAMURTI

In Spain his books were burnt.

Up until 1939. He made several trips to India and spoke to many audiences. He met Gandhi on a number of occasions - whom he respected, but did not admire.

California. At the outbreak of the Second World War, **K** found himself in Ojai, where he has spent eight years in relative isolation, accompanied only by Rajagopal and his wife.

Despite his file at the CIA, K managed to extend his visa. But because of his pacifism, and his openness in introducing the theme of the 'conscientious objector' he was forbidden to give talks in the US. The devastation wrought by the atomic bomb filled him with extreme horror, but at the same time brought him intense perceptions about the nature of violence and evil.

K liked to walk in silence in the mountains that surround the valley of Ojai. He walked a great deal. He spent entire days alone, forgetting even to eat, exploring and listening to his interior world and to the one surrounding him...

...he tended the garden, grew roses and vegetables, washed dishes, tidied and cleaned the house. Every day he meditated for an hour while listening to Beethoven's Ninth Symphony. In the afternoon he chanted hymns in Sanskrit which he remembered from his early childhood.

When he wrote in his **Journal** * he referred to himself in the third person:

He only discovered recently that there was not a single thought during these long walks, in the crowded street or on the solitary paths. Ever since he was a boy it had been like that, no thought entered his mind. He was watching and listening and nothing else. Thought with its associations never arose. There was no image-making. One day he was suddenly aware how extraordinary it was; he attempted often to think but no thought would come. on these walks, with people or without them, any movement of thought was absent. This is to be alone.

He always had this strange lack of distance between himself and the trees, rivers and mountains. It wasn't cultivated: you can't cultivate a thing like that. There was never a wall between him and another. What they did to him, what they said to him never seemed to wound him, nor flattery to touch him. Somehow he was altogether untouched. He was not withdrawn, aloof but like the waters of a river. He had so few thoughts; no thoughts at all when he was alone. His brain was active when talking or writing but otherwise it was quiet and active without movement. Movement is time and activity is not.

***** Krishnamurti's Journal, Gollancz, 1982***

Greta Garbo, Charlie Chaplin, Bertrand Russell and other actors, researchers and philosophers gathered round him and visited him very often. However, with a certain English biologist, who was practically blind, **K** established a deep friendship : **Aldous Huxley**. They were both studying the circumstances in which the mind becomes creative.

Through his family tradition, Huxley was a 'generalist': he knew a lot about many things. However, he was prepared to give up all his knowledge in exchange for a mystic experience such as **K** had had. He could only reach those states of Oneness through using a particular drug. When Huxley became very intellectual, **K** said not a word. He stayed near him and established a strong - for both of them - non-verbal communication.

1944. In spite of the war, when **K** spoke in public, people turned up from all over the USA. One Sunday, he gave a talk in the Oakwood of Ojai.

The War . That did not leave him untouched. After the German invasion of Holland, the Ommen Camp, where his European meetings used to be celebrated, was converted into a concentration camp. Many of his European friends had to emigrate . The USA seemed to be asleep. Material survival became difficult everywhere. **K** wrote to Lady Emily, who had already lost two grandsons at the front.

Writing. He didn't write to publish books. The only works he wrote himself were **"Commentaries on Living"** and **'Journals I & II'**. The rest (over a hundred) were transcriptions of his talks and conversations. Huxley not only encouraged him to write, but to a certain extent became the imaginary questioner in his texts.

Why do you refuse to write regularly?

Using the thought-memory to write is to focus it on the past, on that which no longer exists. Thus you are not aware.

What does that mean - to be aware?

OBVIOUS AWARENESS

ACTIVE AWARENESS

THOUGHTFUL AWARENESS

If you look into your mind you will see thousands of butterflies fluttering their wings. It is impossible to grasp their complexity. But if you look attentively at just one butterfly you will gradually come to understand the others.

William Quinn, the young man who posed these questions, participated, years later, in setting up the **Esalen Institute** in Big Sur, the birthplace of the **Movement for Human Potential** and of **Gestalt**. At this moment, being with **K**, the boy discovered that confusion in the mind came from his repetitive thoughts that remained unresolved. This 'awareness' would change the thinking of young people in the generations to come, driving a wedge into traditional psychology.

1945. During the First World War, **K** maintained a lyrical optimism. In spite of many people writing to him and confessing that reading his book **"Education and the Significance of Life'** had brought about peaceful yet irreversible revolutions, the Second World War left a disillusioned look in his eyes.

At the end of the war, **K** fell seriously ill. He suffered from a urinary infection, with a high temperature and remained unconscious for long periods of time. The doctors were unable to diagnose his illness and could not prescribe him anything. One day he mysteriously recovered. Doctors were dumbfounded; he attributed his cure to his own spiritual regime.

1946. Erich Fromm, Karen Horney, Benjamin Weinniger and other important psychologists from New York and Washington found similarities between **K**'s teachings and their own schools of therapy. What happened when he was invited to give a talk was more instructive than the explanation itself.

The same year a small secondary school was opened in Ojai Valley, on the land bought by Annie Besant for this purpose twenty years before. It was called **Happy Valley School**.

III. Creative perception

India, 16th August, 1947.
India's Independence is declared. **K** decided to apply for an Indian passport and not renew his British one. Two months later he moved to India, where he stayed a year and a half. It was the first time he arrived on his own. There was nobody to organise activities for him nor to decide whom he should see or where he should go. He felt completely free; in his mind as much as in his body.

The young people who gathered round **K** came from several disciplines: politics, literature, sociology and sciences. In Bombay a new group of followers was formed, in which two brothers stood out. **Pupul Jayakar** and **Nandini Metha**. **K** used dialogue as the principal means of exploration. He didn't mind if they didn't understand what he said. He managed to arouse their interest.

Political and social action can change the world. Patriotism leads to happiness.
Systems can never transform men. It is they who always change the system. As I told you a year ago, creative thought is needed.
What is 'creative thought'?
Seeing and listening to reality as it is. Not as it should be.
With the creation of the state of Pakistan, the partition of India was completed. A little later, violence broke out between Hindus and Muslims, leading to enormous bloodshed.

BANG
1948. On the 30th January, Gandhi was assasinated. During an hour and a half Jawaharlal Nehru shared his solitatary anguish with K and his extreme concern about the violence that has broken out since Independence.
In India two forces are at work: the forces of good and those of evil.
What should we think? What should we do?
Good and evil are always present.
For now, a few individuals should free themselves from the elements that are corrupting humankind. Only when we think creatively will those individuals be able to change the lives of all the rest.

For **K**, the chaos of the world was a projection of the individual's own chaos. It all had to do with the difficulty of dying and being born again at every instant. **Pupul Jayakar** and her mother – still grieving over her husband's death – had a conversation with K, from which emerged the sense of urgency to escape the traps that sentiment can lead to.

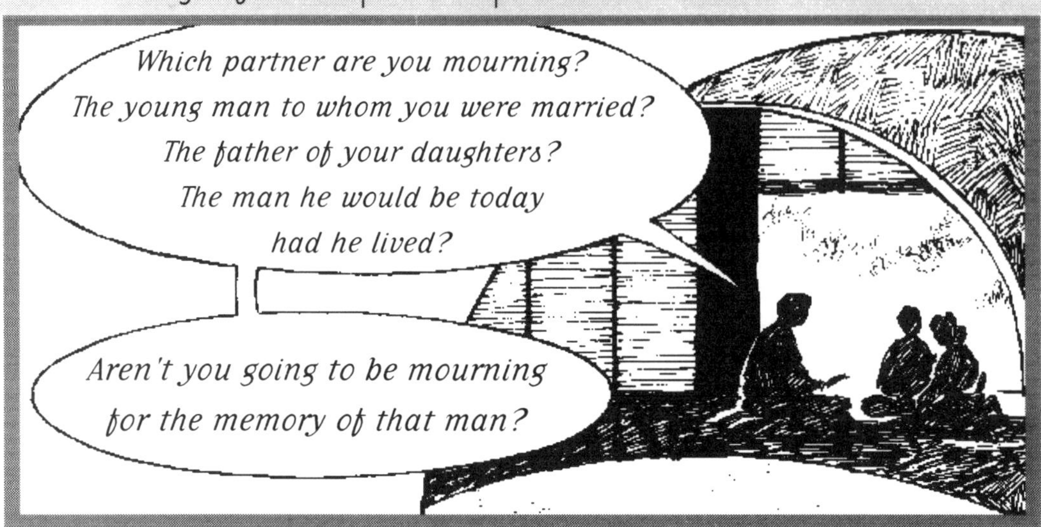

Then, when Pupul told him that she would give herself over to social work, **K** burst out laughing and compared such an enterprise to lifting water from a well with a bucket full of holes. *'The more you take up, the more you lose.'* In the biography of K that Pupul had yet to write, having worked with him for thirty years, she has recorded that, in such moments ...

Madras. K decided to rest a while. But no sooner had he installed himself in a secluded villa, than the 'process' began again, whereby his body once more became 'occupied' by a 'higher' presence. One morning he asked Pupul and Nandini to wait at home for him, while he went out walking by himself. On his return he seemed different.
In a small way. I have not returned. They have set fire to me so as to leave a greater emptiness.
Pupul and Nandini felt that a vibrancy, strange and at once sacred, had invaded the room. During two of the six weeks they passed in their mountain retreat, **K** had been in contact with those forces.

1949-56. K went back to Ojai and decided to extend his time there. For a year he gave no talks nor interviews. In total silence, he turned his gaze upon himself. He developed a friendship with Vanda Passigli de Scaravelli, in whose country estate, among olive trees and cypresses, surrounded by hills, he could find some refuge from his constant travels between Ojai and India.

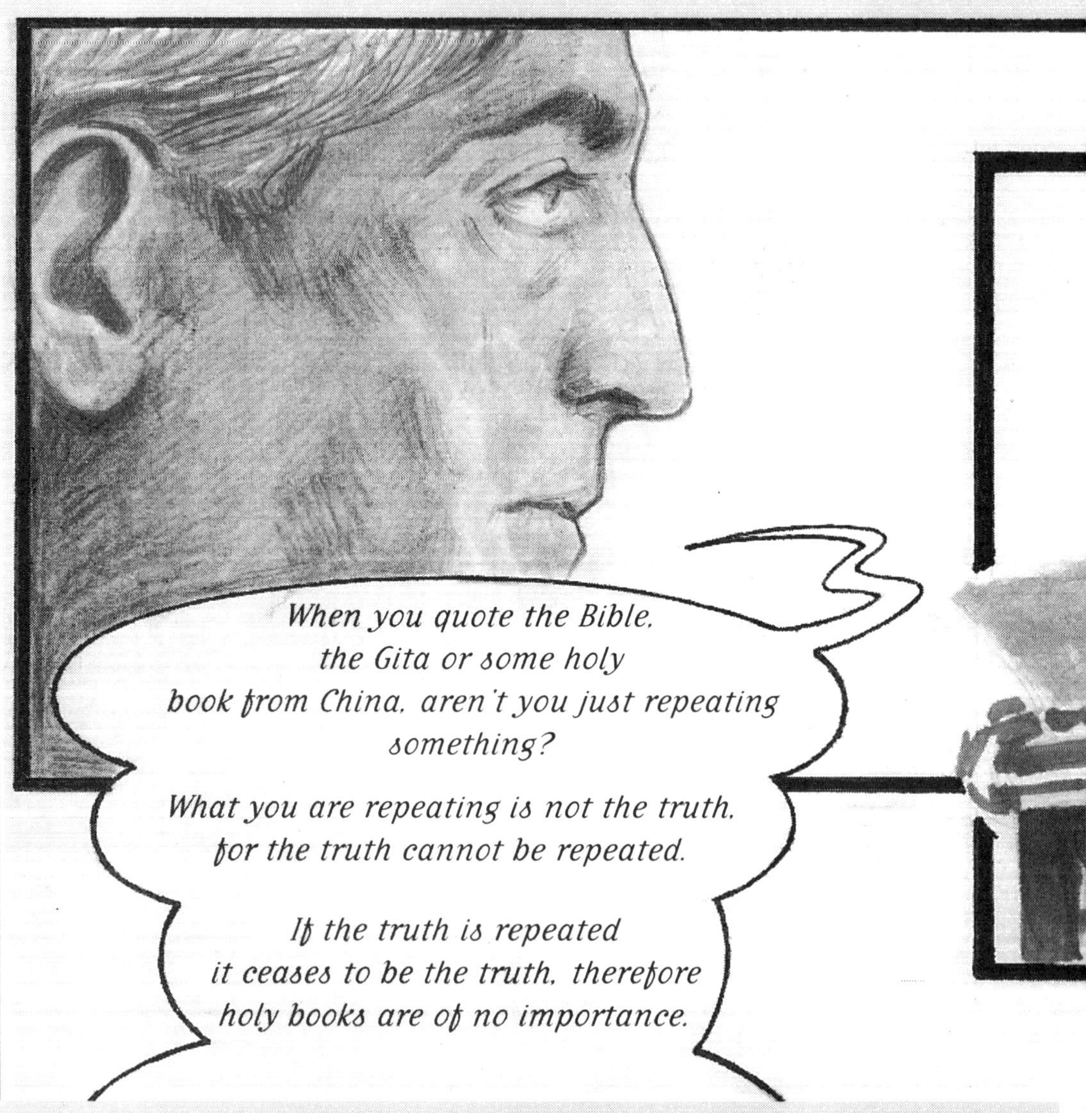

K judged that only through one's own knowledge, rather than through belief in other people's symbols, could one reach the everlasting reality that is rooted in one's own being.

In **1953 K**'s first book came out – **Education and the Meaning of Life** – and three years later the second – **First and Last Reality**. With a lengthy introduction by **Aldous Huxley,** the second book attracted more people to **K**'s teachings than any previous publication.

To free himself from belief, K never read any more sacred books.

We must be content with reading newspapers, magazines and detective stories. That means that we can be faced with the crisis of our times, not with love or understanding, but with formulas and systems, which are not of much value in rigorous terms. Formulas lead to 'the blindness of thought'.

We are educated to be members of one group
or another, be it Communist, Christian,
Buddhist or Freudian.
And so we respond with old
standards, without originality nor
freshness.
And our response is worthless.

Three big ideas on leadership
1. The very idea of leading the masses is antisocial and antispiritual. 2. The leader feels satisfied in his desire for power, and those who allow themselves to be led by him feel satisfied in their desire for certainty and security. 3. A spiritual guide bestows a kind of narcosis on his disciples.
Maybe you too behave like a spiritual guide.
I can bring you no satisfaction. I do not tell you what you should be doing every minute. I simply give signals. I tell you: this is a fact, you can take it or leave it. Most people reject that, for the simple reason that the fact is not going to bring satisfaction.

If, as Huxley wondered, K could offer no belief system, no catalogue of dogmas, no inventory of ideas or ideals ... If he was not interested in any kind of dictatorship, no mediation nor spiritual direction, not even some kind of example, such as ritual, a church, a code of some sort of pep talk ... If he would not suggest introspection, self analysis, nor a set of consecrated principles ...

Treasure

Inner freedom has to be discovered, to be lived through ... It is a state of being, like silence, in which there is no becoming, in which there is only fullness. It does not necessarily have to seek expression. It is not a talent that requires exterior manifestation. It is not a gift, nor does it result from any skill.

A.M. Lindbergh, author of the classic ***Lord of the Sea***, remarked that **K** had, in a single paragraph of one of his reported lectures, given the reader enough confidence to undertake several days of exploration, questioning and reflection.

1956. Commentaries on Life, K's third book, appeared. Personal interviews were transcribed in it. In a short time the Governor of Ceylon (today Sri Lanka) allowed five of K's lectures to be broadcast. He was going through a crisis in his relationship with his secretary, Rajagopal. His travels were arranged by Doris Pratt, in charge of **Krishnamurti Writings**, based in London. From her office in Wimbledon, she organised meetings which were, for the first time, recorded on tape.

Who is the master?
In his talks to young people and schoolmasters, K was questioning knowledge of the development of humankind.
The school has to protect and keep teaching alive. given the extent of disorder and violence in the world.
So teachers and students need to be equipped with ears to listen and eyes to see with the broadest understanding. with no identification nor fragmentation.
In these conversations, which would be published as Krishnamurti and Education, key responses were called for: a permanent revolution.

Conferences. The first meeting, held in the Swiss town of Saanen, attracted people from all over the world. The conferences were repeated annually. In the following 24 years the programme became an international event. On one occasion, **K** met the South African pianist Alain Naudé, who would become his secretary for several years. **K** was already aged 70 and he found it difficult to travel alone. Mary Zimbalist, widow of the film maker and a businesswoman, also accompanied **K** on his journeys.

IV. Krishnamurti's living thoughts

Basic themes

In the years that followed, **K** returned to the same basic themes in all of his conversations. However, he did not always use the same precise terms. All of his work was aimed at producing a radical transformation in the mind of anyone listening to him or reading his words. **K** was convinced that without such a transformation there could be no real shift in the ways of society, no peace and joy in the world.

Between yourselves and those who speak with you

With this sort of expression, **K** instilled in his listeners the notion that each of his talks was more of a conversation than a lecture.

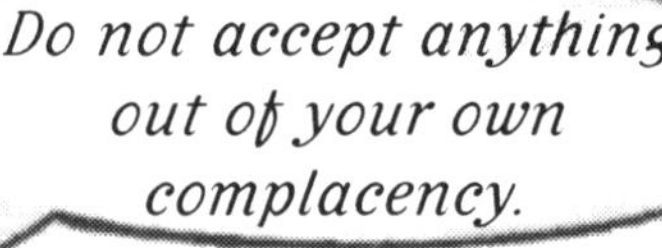

Right thinking. It is essential not to cling to any past experience, whether it be national, religious or personal. Before being able to act, we have to learn to think. Without true ideas of our own, there is no action. Thoughtless actions have led us into this confusion, this world crisis. Knowing oneself is not fleeing from this life and this world.

We are the world. The world's problem is our problem – that is something which is at once an individual and a world crisis.

One man cannot change the world, but you yourselves, together with me, can indeed change the world. You and I can find that notion to be true, because truth dispenses with the sufferings and the sorrows of this world.

A real revolution is not a bloody one, rather a revolution of internal regeneration. And there can be no regeneration without self knowledge.

Understanding with no excess. To perceive the truth at the crossroads of one problem and another, we have to take stock of that, without the scars of yesterday's memories.

Once having identified whatever is left over, in excess, from that moment of understanding, we find we can be rid of it with no resistance. We find that the mind is refreshed, so as to discover the truth, all at once ...

Understanding is not a continuous thread. It does not lead from moment to moment. It does not leave anything behind – no excess – nothing remains. To 'receive' the truth, its beauty and its joy, it is necessary to have an 'instant grasp', unclouded by theories, by fears, by received notions.

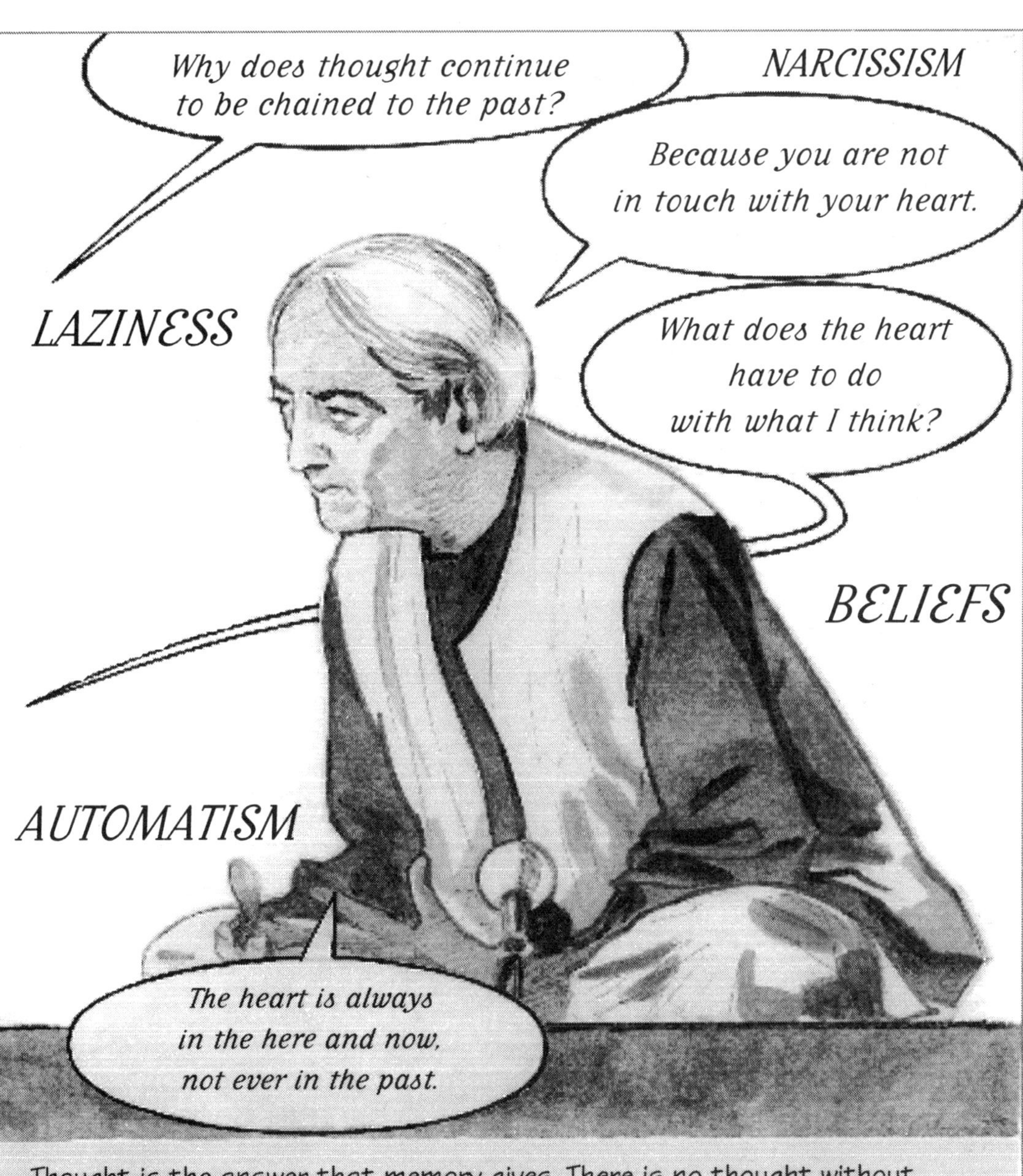

Thought is the answer that memory gives. There is no thought without the past. Memory is the rediscovery of incomplete experience that has not been altogether understood. That incomplete experience, which people call memory, gives rise to thought. Ideas arise from thought.

Thought splits the mind from the heart. The mind, with its roots in egocentric activity, is conducive to an increase in material values and to a slow withering of all the intents and purposes that can nourish the true human condition.

Finishing with thought. What if thought is not the highest form of intelligence? What do we really mean by finishing with thought? Is thought indispensable? Should we be going further than that?

When thought takes over, the past comes alive in the present, shifting its shape within itself and in the present also. Consequently, there is nothing new in it, nothing vital. If we want to find something new, the past has to find itself somewhere else. The mind cannot be obstructed by thought, by fear, by contentment – not by any such things. Only when the mind is free of confusion can anything new manifest itself.

For this reason, we have to say that thought must be silent, happening only when it has to, in an objective way, efficiently. Wherever there is continuity, there can be nothing new.

K said that there is something sacred which does not come from thought. And it is not a feeling that can be revived by thought. Thought cannot recognise it, cannot use it, cannot formulate it. It cannot be communicated.

On other occasions, K said that thought is contaminated, that it is corrupted, that thought is corrupt because it is divided, fragmented. K was referring to ***psychological thought***. But, at any rate, he considered thought to be necessary for memory and all practical purposes.

Psychological processes. K held the view that true understanding could be obtained only through complete consciousness of the mind and its images. These are reflected continuously in the connections that one can forge with others. To advance to this state and to free oneself, it is necessary to follow these steps:

1. Consciousness

This is a state of total concentration in which the mind does not fight nor focus itself, nor form impressions, nor analyse anything: it does not even think. This is the true state of meditation.

2. Thought

Memories, apprehensions and accumulated experiences have their origin in conditioning or in past reactions. It is *thought* that gives rise to the idea of who the 'self' is. For consciousness to function freely, thought has to remain in silence and stillness.

3. Imagination

Images, opinions, ideas and preconceived notions distort our perceptions of reality. Such images press one to compare oneself with other people. Between oneself and others, those images create psychological and cultural barriers. Just as with *thought*, images will fall way when one observes oneself in an unconditional way.

4. Conditioning

Each person's *formation* (the characteristics acquired by an individual's personality) must be the result of past experiences and thoughts. The only way to go beyond this is through consciousness and acceptance of 'who and what one is', without making any choices.

5. Knowledge and learning

We give the name *knowledge* to thoughts and images from the past. These are incapable of bringing anything new to the reality of being. *Learning* is a state activated and defined by *doing*. It is possible to arrive at this by means of the consciousness being freed of presuppositions.

6. Fears, memories ad dependencies

Pleasures, pains and ties arise from past experiences. By looking continually for pleasure, the mind invites sorrow in. This prolongs the fear of losing pleasure. Only when thought no longer interferes can fear be understood.

7. Conflict

The divisive nature of thought can result in alienation and violence. K rejected any violent reactions, be they wars or any conflict between people.

8. The capacity to relate

Understanding of one's own being arises from total unification of the physical with the psychological. Thought destroys relations. Relations can be kept alive only through a state of full consciousness.

9. Intelligence

The capacity to see 'who and what one is' – true intelligence – is not linked to the rational faculty of thinking, of thought. True intelligence exists only by virtue of harmony and 'quietude' of the mind. It enables a person to be freed from thought, without generating any conflict or violence.

Death in life is life without death. Death signifies an end to attachments. We have to die whilst we are alive, without waiting for some illness to put an end to us.

Death implies and infers living with all our vitality, our energy, our intellectual capacity, and with a great feeling for all things. At the same time, death means finishing with idiosyncrasies, experiences, attachments, psychological wounds. It means dying for all of that.

One is humanity. The content of our consciousness is common to all humanity. We are not individuals. We are not separate souls, with psychological elements that are set apart, struggling to obtain something.

Every one of us is the rest of humanity.

Many searchers after truth do confirm it ...

... they confirm it, they have confirmed it, they will confirm it.

It is not possible to be deeply attentive if one is at all fearful ...
One cannot wonder ... nor be observant ...
nor can one learn.
Fear. Living is finding for oneself what the truth might be. Only when freedom can be enjoyed can that truth be found, when there is a perpetual revolution deep within oneself. Truth, whether it be God or love, can be found if one constantly observes and learns, constantly questioning oneself. The truth, God or love, will make itself known.

Human relations and fellowship. To communicate ideas is relatively easy. But to achieve fellowship, communion, one with another, above the level of words – that is an extremely arduous task. To commune one with another, we need to be open and receptive – not to accept nor to deny, but to inquire.

We are related – we do not live in isolation. Truth is not something separate from interrelations. Interrelation is society. If any of you can understand your relationship with your partner, if you understand the relationship between yourselves and society, you will find the truth.

Does a couple's relationship unite them?
If everybody pursues their own desires and ambitions, with covetousness, how can there be any relationships
Could meditating together be helpful?
!
A relationship is the most difficult thing in life.

Meditation is not an end in itself. Meditation cannot solely consist of disciplining mind and heart in accord with some determined model. It is a process of endless understanding, from moment to moment.
Understanding arises only when there is some perception
... not of some abstract truth but of the truth of existence.
Aha!
But – who amongst us can perceive accurately?

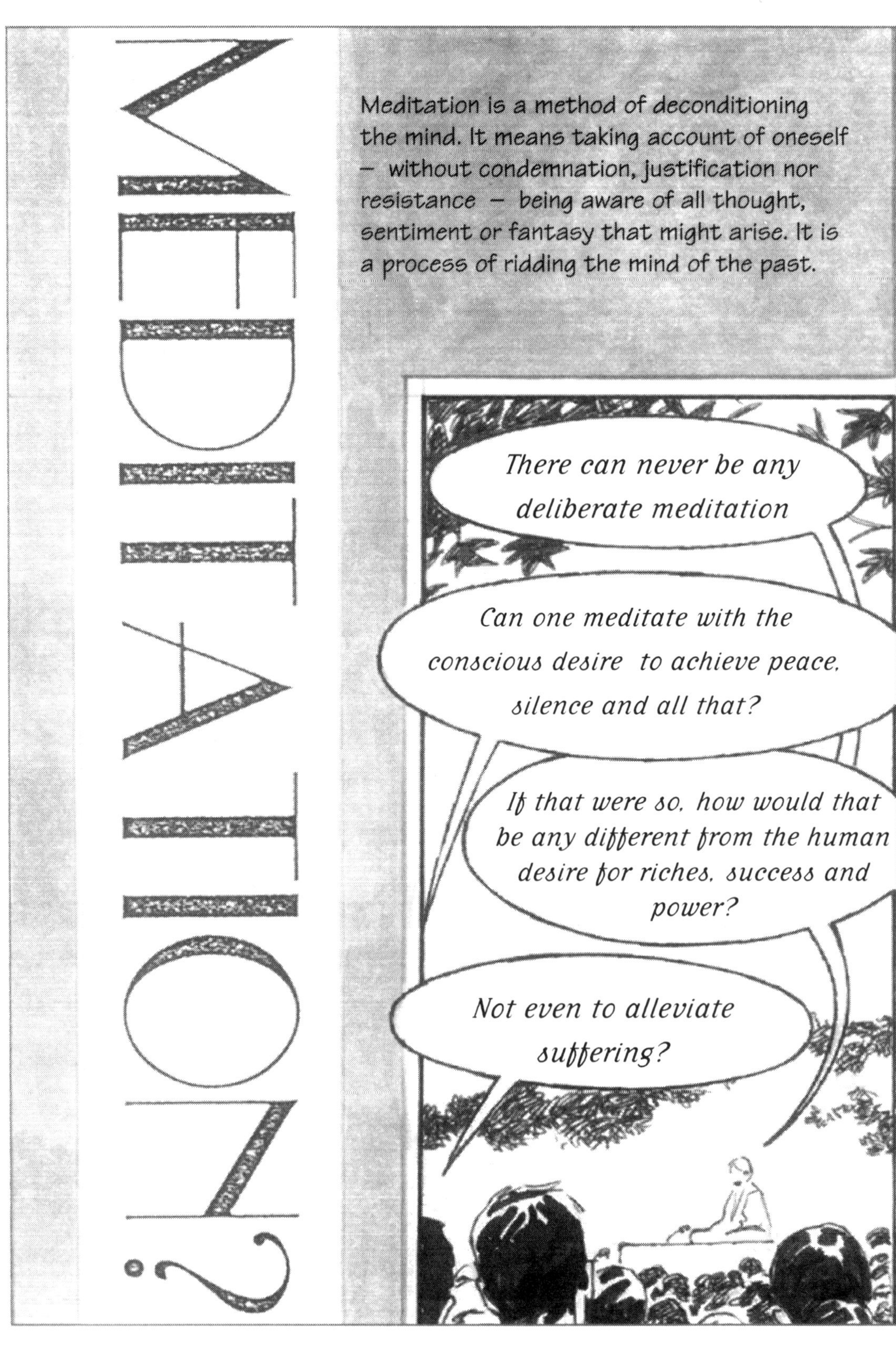
MEDITATION?
Meditation is a method of deconditioning the mind. It means taking account of oneself — without condemnation, justification nor resistance — being aware of all thought, sentiment or fantasy that might arise. It is a process of ridding the mind of the past.
There can never be any deliberate meditation
Can one meditate with the conscious desire to achieve peace, silence and all that?
If that were so, how would that be any different from the human desire for riches, success and power?
Not even to alleviate suffering?

Suffering. Suffering is our common lot. There is no point in being content to evade suffering. Nothing can be understood by avoiding it without loving it and penetrating it.

For a person who is happy, who is capable of love, there is no divisiveness. When the heart is full, things of the mind wither away.

Love has no need of philosophy.
When one can love, life is more simple.
One's heart goes out to everything and everybody ...
... it finds itself in a state of sensibility, of flexibility.
Love is not something that can be cultivated. It arises directly and speedily, when one is not being hampered by things of the mind. If there is love – that fervour, benevolence, pity – there is no need for philosophy, for teachings, because love is its own truth.
To understand, you must have love in your heart.

Love is that state in which thought processes, functioning through time, have ceased completely. Where there is love, there is transformation. Love is no different from the truth. Denial of love is a destructive tendency, present in humankind. Humanity can flourish only when the mind makes a settlement with the heart, and when there is complete denial of egocentric activity.

People who love are dangerous and we do not wish to live dangerously. We wish to live efficiently, within organisational frameworks, because we are deluded into believing that organisations will bring peace and order to the world.

Integrated action

When we want to resolve a problem at its own proper level, as if there were no connection with other problems in our lives, this process is nothing but mere activity. Activity is the kind of action that is unrelated to the crossroads where the problem arises. Humankind does not live only at one level but at different levels of consciousness. The act of separating our lives into compartments, at different levels that have no relation to one another, is detrimental to action. Activity is the result of an idea. It is always a means to isolation, not to unification.

Integrated action is not born of an idea. It arises when we understand our lives as an all embracing process, consisting of separate activities, distinct from the totality of existence. Integrated action is action with no basis in ideas. It is understanding the total process. One's own understanding is a requirement for being able to act in an integrated way. One's own understanding is not an idea

Negative thought. In order to perceive everything, the mind must remain in absolute silence. But that silence, that 'quietude', is not induced nor produced by discipline and control. It happens when the mind is aware of all distractions, when they are made to cease.

Do not force yourselves to find tranquillity.

Do not try to discipline the mind.

Or else you will never perceive the problem as a whole.

The loss of religion. Religion is a way of searching after truth and reality, not of surrounding oneself with substitutes and false values. The quest for reality is not a question of a journey to a faraway place, for reality is very close by. It lies in what is to be done, thought and felt. We want to have beliefs, dogmas, security. So, as a wealthy person seeks security in pictures and precious stones, many look for safety in organised religion.

Learning. The flame is lit by investigation, by our looking at ourselves, by learning closely about ourselves. Learning is not the same as acquiring knowledge.

Learning signifies undistorted observation, seeing things as they are. It is not an accumulative process, because it takes place in movement.

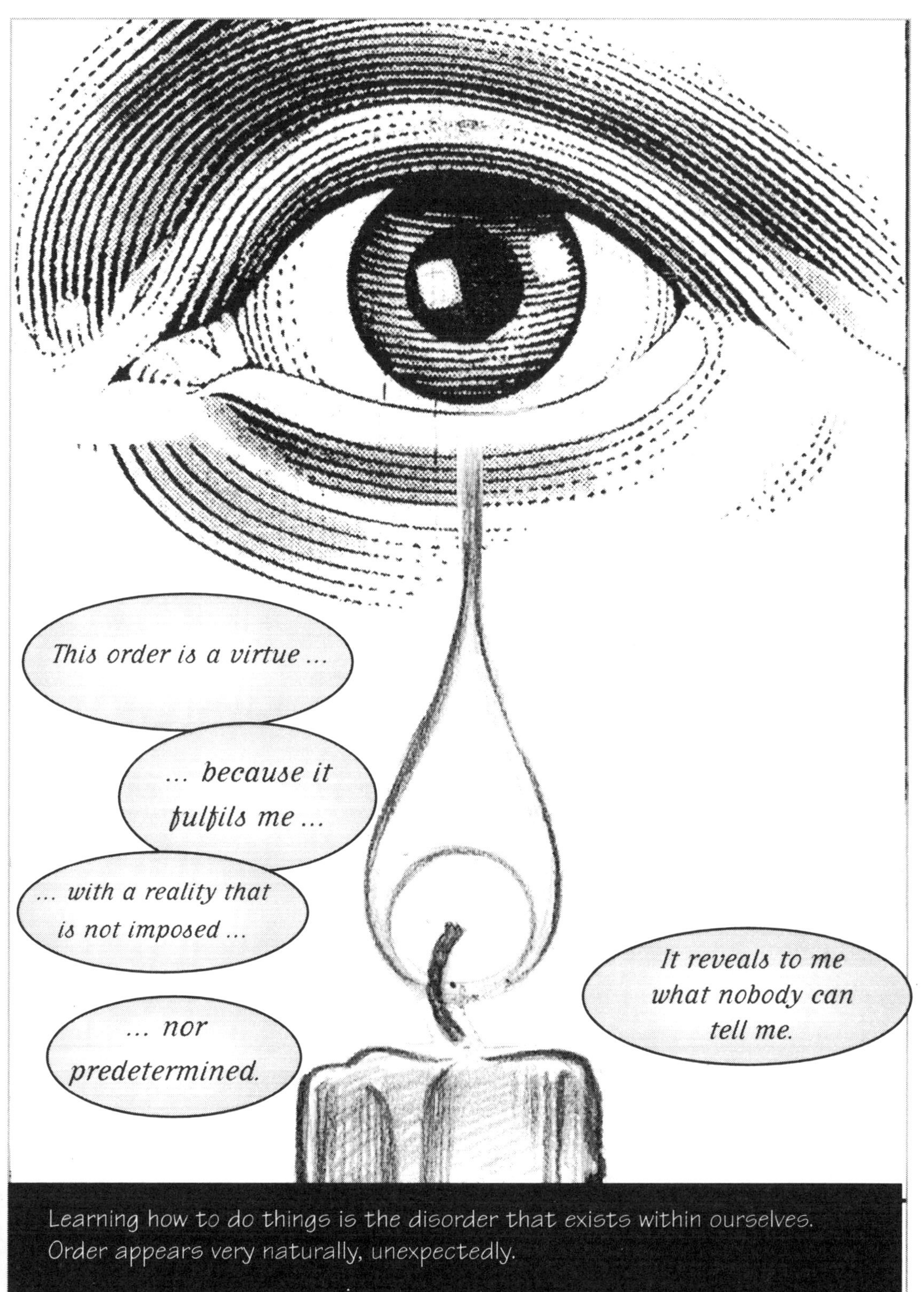
This order is a virtue ...
... because it fulfils me ...
... with a reality that is not imposed ...
... nor predetermined.
It reveals to me what nobody can tell me.
Learning how to do things is the disorder that exists within ourselves. Order appears very naturally, unexpectedly.

Education systems. These have failed completely throughout the world, because there is something radically mistaken about the way we educate our children.
If our objective is to produce efficient machines, it is obvious that we need a system.
But systems can produce machines only by way of certain responses. No system can manufacture individuals with an an alert state of mind.
For this reason, our own civilisation is destroying itself.
TURN TO A PLACE OF FREEDOM PG. 125

The difficulty lies in that modern education teaches a child that it ought to think, instead of teaching it how to think. Life can be faced only when one has the capacity to think intelligently. Just as our children are taught to think in fragmented ways, so they do not become integrated beings.

It is not possible to educate a child so as to become an integrated individual if one does not understand the integration of one's own self.

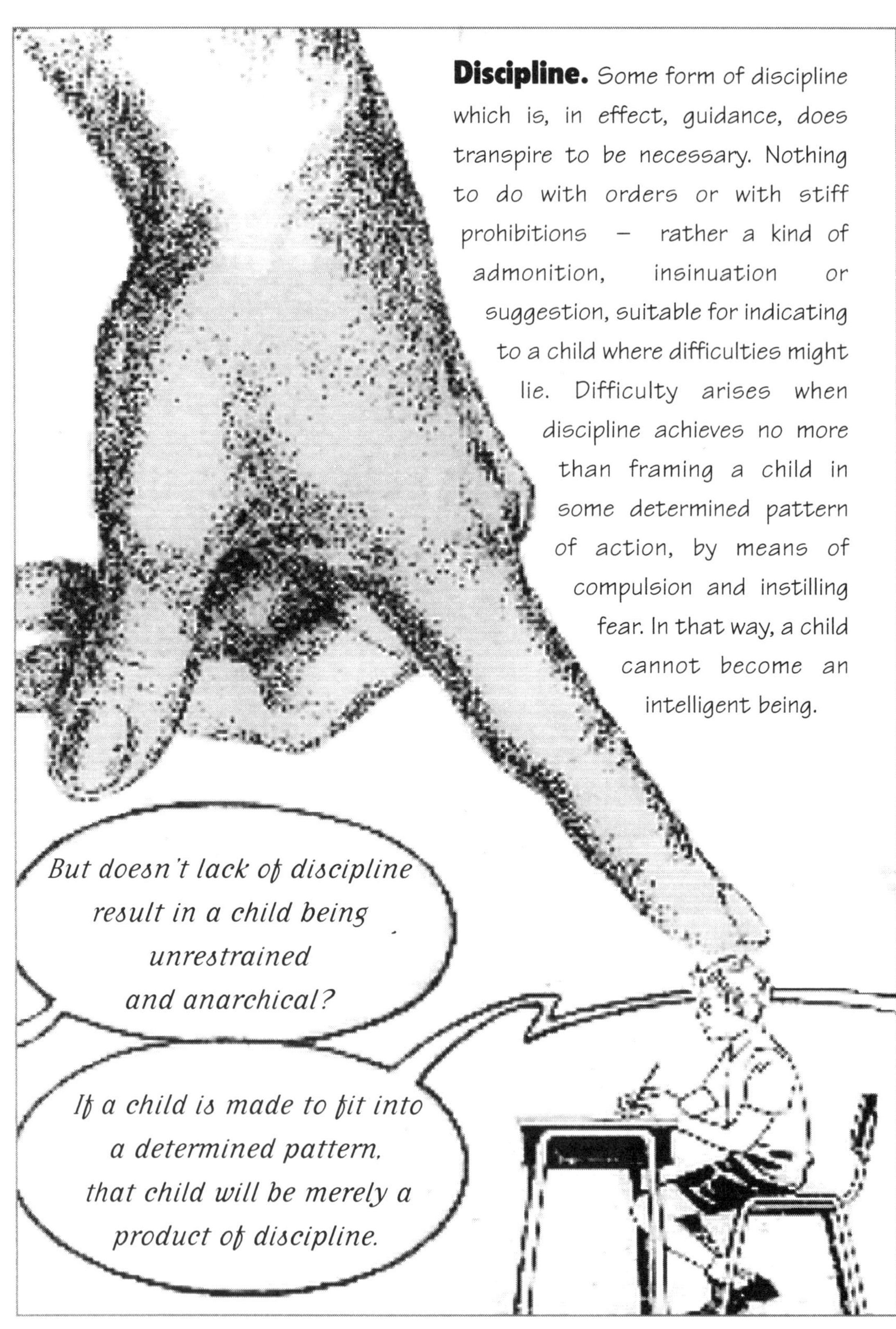
Discipline. Some form of discipline which is, in effect, guidance, does transpire to be necessary. Nothing to do with orders or with stiff prohibitions – rather a kind of admonition, insinuation or suggestion, suitable for indicating to a child where difficulties might lie. Difficulty arises when discipline achieves no more than framing a child in some determined pattern of action, by means of compulsion and instilling fear. In that way, a child cannot become an intelligent being.
But doesn't lack of discipline result in a child being unrestrained and anarchical?
If a child is made to fit into a determined pattern, that child will be merely a product of discipline.

True education is the creation of intelligence. That is not to be achieved by means of mass education. Rather the means to be employed is by considering each child carefully, with affection, studying the child's difficulties, idiosyncrasies and capacities.
When the heart is open, discipline takes the role of affection ...
... and gives way to the need to fill the heart with something.
Necessity for invention!
That way we shall have invented God!

God. The liveliness of reality is not a matter of belief. Somebody who does believe in that must be without knowledge of it and, in speaking of it, does no more than play with words. But reality is not to be measured. It cannot be captured by a string of words.

Through lack of intelligence we accept the idea of a superintelligence that we call God. But that God is not about to bestow a better life on us. It is intelligence that leads us to a better life. There can be no intelligence whilst there is belief, whilst there are class divisions, whilst the means of production remain in the hands of a few, whilst there are nationalities etc. All of that shows lack of intelligence. That is what hinders us in living a better life, not the decision not to believe in God.

Freedom. Man is never free; overwhelmed as he is by his own experience or knowledge, because this knowledge stops him from learning. If he wants to find out what freedom is, and discover its beauty, its immensity and its energy, he must start by giving up any commitments or the desire for belonging to something.

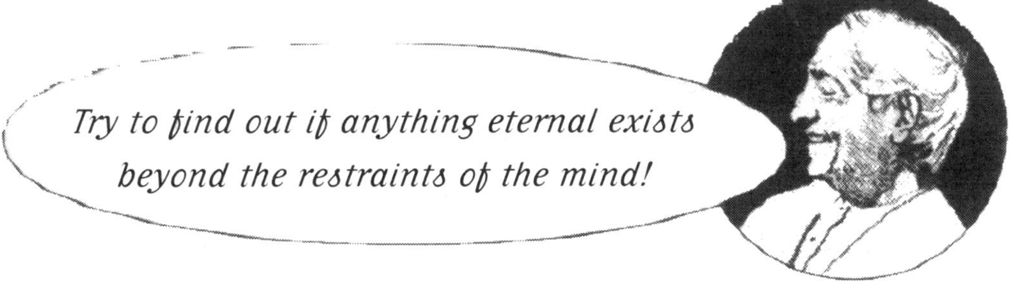

Try to find out if anything eternal exists beyond the restraints of the mind!

Man boasts that he's free because he has freedom of choice. Freedom doesn't have an aim; you don't find it at the final stage of man's evolution. It's there in the first step of his existence. We become aware of the absence of freedom through observation. We find freedom in our daily life through our observations and without needing to choose.

Freedom is pure undirected observation, without fear hiding itself behind punishments or rewards.

Transformation. It's something very simple: to see wrong as wrong and truth as truth. Also to see the true in the false, and see the false in what has been accepted as truth. Because when we see very clearly that something is true, that truth is liberating. The very perception of truth is transformation, and as we are surrounded by so many lies, suddenly to be aware of the lie is transformation.

Every act that has changed man fundamentally has come from another human being. The transformation of the individual isn't a gradual process. It's instantaneous, it happens when man looks in the mirror and sees how he relates to other men, to nature and to himself.

East and West Apparently, the Indian character has from the beginning of time always had something genuine, true. Indians were profoundly religious in the true sense of the word. Does the world of today with astrologers and gurus suggest that this depth of character is exhausted?

Is that religious core now disappearing? If it does still exist, how are the West and its values responding? On the other hand, if the core or nucleus has disappeared in India, are the East and West becoming more similar?

Hindu thought puts an emphasis on scepticism. Scepticism, with its clarity and immense vitality, clears illusions from the mind. Is India losing its scepticism? Is doubt being replaced by faith? Is India joining Western fashion?

Desire. Observing the process of desire in myself, I see that my mind is always moving towards an object in search of more sensation, and that resistance, temptation and discipline become involved. The mind automatically takes us through perception, sensation, contact and desire. In this process the symbols, words and objects are the centre around which all desire, obligations and ambitions stand out; that centre is the Self.

The problem of sexuality. Every time that someone asked his opinion about the chaos that sex creates in many men and women's personal lives - is it a physical need? a psychological need? - , **K** saw the mind as the source of the problem. He considered that conditioning to be highly exaggerated.

The Second Act: The Explanation
Everything I do gives me pleasure: my business, my religion, my political activities, my social involvement.
That's what you think. All of that accentuates and gives strength to your "Self". The only escape route is that moment of sexual pleasure when you forget about yourself and you believe you're happy.
I also get happiness by other means.
We're talking about a happiness that conceals suffering.
Let's say we agree. The problem is...

K's own life demonstrates that living in a state of wholeness is a blessing, because it results in forgetting the self, and losing the reaction of the "Self". This isn't an abstract response to the daily problem of sex, it is the only answer. The mind doesn't know love, and without love there's no chastity. When there's love, sex doesn't become a problem. The problem is not one of sex but of education; we should bring up children not by forbidding them excitement but by getting them used to forgetting their "Self".

V. A Place of Freedom

The purpose of education

Every year **K** visited the schools established in India, particularly the one at **Rajghat**, in Benares (1948) and the one in the **Rishi Valley** in Andra Pradesh. The Rajghat school, the **Besant** College and the **Agricultural School** formed an extraordinarily beautiful campus where the Varuna and Ganges rivers met. That wonderful position had been chosen by the British army as a resting place for its officers. After the tireless efforts of a teacher, **Shiva Rao** and many years of negotiation, the property was bought in the name of the Rishi Valley Trust. The complex included the school buildings, large dormitories and communal dining rooms, a magnificent auditorium, a post office, an antique Hindu temple with stairways leading to the Ganges and a Muslim mosque facing the River Varuna.

"My teachings need a new generation, a new state of mind. They need the teacher and the student to know how to listen and have far-reaching vision, without identification or fragmentation. There should be a sense of wholeness in the student and the master; a flowering, growing, an extraordinary sense of the holy. There should be truthfulness and an absence of fear. The child should be in direct contact with the earth."

In **1968, in Brockwood Park**, in Hampshire, **K** established a centre of learning for young people of both sexes between thirteen and nineteen years old. **K** lived there when he came to England. Twice a week he gave talks and held informal discussions with the students, teachers and staff of the centre; he also met the parents.

"Our problem about education, is how to keep our energy going, to give it greater vitality, a more dynamic force... How to increase it, how to help it become independent and continuous, in such a way that it becomes the movement towards truth, towards God. Moving towards that which is true, the energy creates waves of a new culture"

K is convinced that most of us are attached to a small part of life and think that, through that part, we'll discover the whole. That through one of its spokes we hope to understand the wheel; but, as he likes to repeat " One spoke does not make a wheel, isn't that right?" He insists that we have to see the whole process of life from childhood if we really want to understand life. And that it is education that must help us to understand the totality of life and not just to prepare us to get work, follow the same old path of marriage, children, security and "the small gods".

Children bloom when....

we help them from babyhood not to imitate others, but to be themselves all the time.

we teach them how to think and not what to think.

we allow them to become free of self-centredness.

we help them to discover life and not take it for granted.

we respect their aware, observant and intensely perceptive minds.

we make learning easier, without too much stress on memorizing.

we take responsibility for their growing up in an aware environment.

we avoid making discipline more important than the people who adhere to it.

and when...

we allow them to learn by making mistakes.

we teach them that those who are most enthusiastic about external change are the ones who ignore the fundamental problems.

we allow fear to rise in them in whatever form; that's the reason that it's indispensable for teachers to understand the roots of their own fear.

we strengthen them so that they never feel damaged psychologically. Not only when they're at school but throughout the rest of their lives.

we stimulate them so that internally, deep inside them, they are in a constant state of rebellion; only those who constantly rebel find truth.

and when...

we cultivate that extraordinary confidence in them that gives them innocence, and prevents them being absorbed into society and losing themselves in mediocrity.

we stop teaching them how to adapt to this corrupt social order and we give them freedom; complete freedom to grow and to create a different society.

they learn to recognise that the difference between useful and destructive knowledge is the principle of intelligence.

they aren't just studying to pass exams.

they can get rid of all the influences that weigh them down and enslave them.

and when...

we educators aren't merely informers, machines imparting a particular piece of knowledge, but we're interested in the well-being of the whole.

we don't interfere with what they really love and want to do; then, from the beginning to the end of their lives they can work at something they feel is worth while and that has real meaning for them.

we encourage them to express their energy and we allow it to take off and sustain itself with force and passion. Only then does the energy become enormous, without limits. If they burn with it, that heat, that energy will grow and produce a new society. It will not dissipate itself in mere rebellions against society as it is, like marks scratched on the walls of a prison.

The true task of education is to make apparent the walls of the prison which enclose our minds.

For **K** education did not end when you're 18 or 21 years old, but when you die. Up to that point, he proposed a path that some considered to be that of the romantic poet. Those who took it knew that when he referred to any kind of truth at other times, he was talking about preparing children for that kind of permanent education.

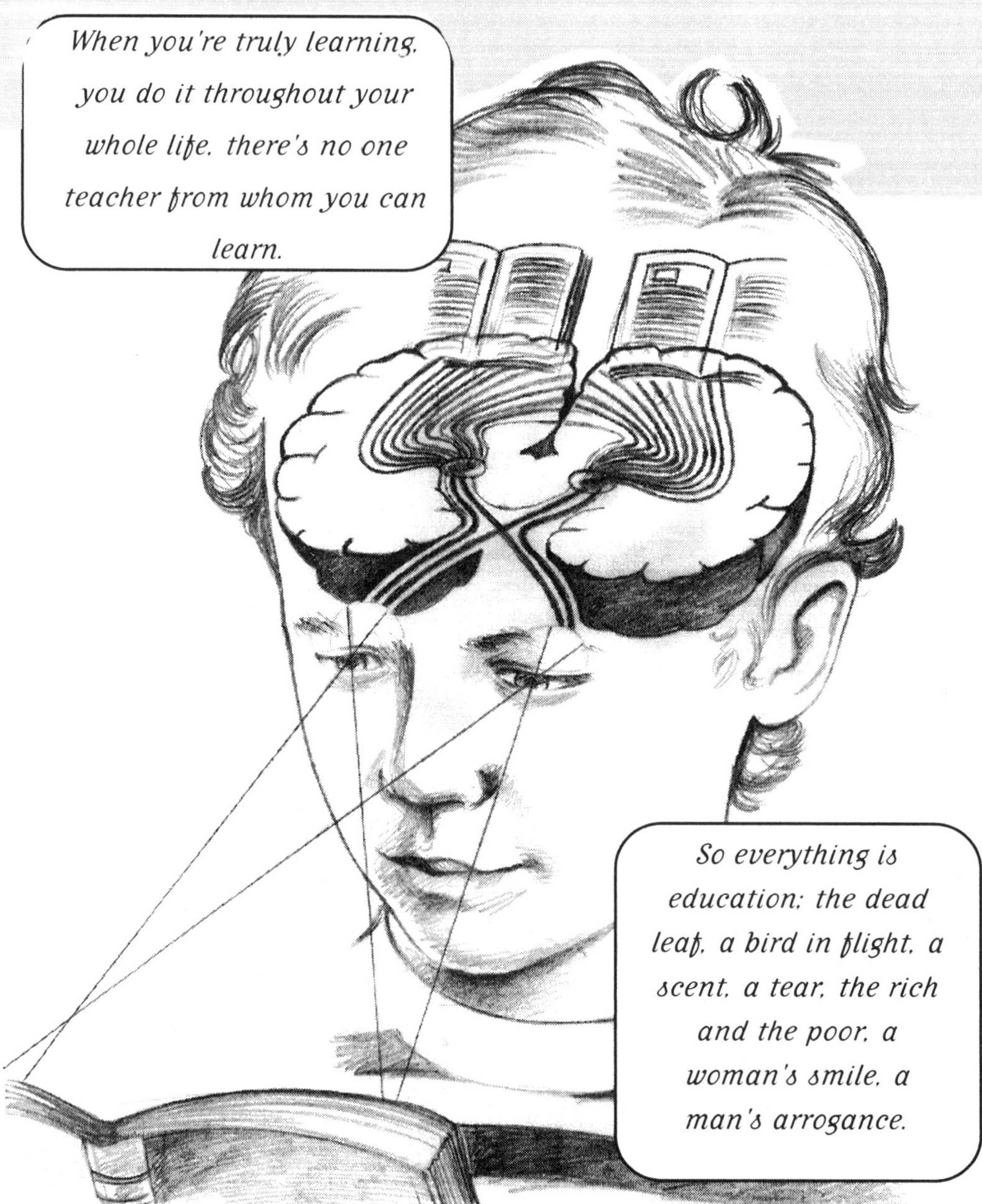

For **K**, this type of active observation was directly linked to listening...

With the help of innumerable examples, **K** always brought his interlocutors to the crucial difference between listening freely, without prejudices or preconceived ideas, and conditioned listening...

K considered that this kind of behaviour, so common to the majority of human beings, is what separated them from life and was the root of much internal pain.

Vi. Mind and thought

India, 1966. **Indira Gandhi** took on the role of prime minister of India until 1977. The following year, the Krishnamurti Foundation of the United States was established, after which there followed a long court case with the **Krishnamurti Writing Inc**. of California. That continued until 1974. The Krishnamurti Foundation of India was also created in 1970. Meanwhile **K** continued his international tours and stayed at Brockwood Park, Malibu and Ojai. The same theme recurred in his talks:

Tensions grew between India and Pakistan. Numbers of refugees reached ten million. **K**'s 'processes' continued, although gentler and without 'out of body' experiences. He rested in Malibu.

Recently **K** had begun to realise that there was one element which was not flowing harmoniously from his writings. The money from his books and the numerous donations didn't appear to be reaching their destination! He asked to be reinstated as director of **Krishnamurti Writing Inc.** under Rajagopal, but was denied access to the accounts, to internal decisions, correspondence and even the archives of his own manuscripts! In July of 1968 **K** broke definitively with Rajagopal. He announced this at the Saanen meeting:.

1972. The first of **K**'s books to come out of India was published: **Tradition and Revolution**, prepared by Pupul Jayakar and Sunanda Patwardhan. Two more of his books also appeared: **Beyond Violence** and **The Awakening of Intelligence**, with 17 photographs. It was the first time that **K** had agreed to photographs being included in his books. **The Awakening...** contained conversations with the philosophy professor, **Jacob Needleman**, with **Swami Venkatesananda, Alain Naude**, and the physicist **David Bohm**, specialist in quantum physics.

During the following years, **K** and Bohm held various conversations. In them, **K** spoke more and more about the end of time and thought.

The scientist and the spiritual teacher use reason to try to build a bridge between their minds.

Bohm accepted that when the mind frees itself from time, it follows that the brain also frees itself from time.

Can we perceive the totality of life if our minds are fragmented? The psychiatrist **David Shainberg** summed up the conversation.

Don't you dare go even further? We're fragmented because we desire security.
Everything that gives us a point of reference helps us to know who we are.
Belonging to something makes us feel secure.
But the price of that security is fragmentation.
GION

What makes us conform to this mechanical lifestyle? And would everything disintegrate if we suddenly stopped conforming in life?
The brain needs total order. Routine gives it that order.
The brain is caught in a trap and it keeps generating disorder. For some reason, it doesn't want to escape from it.
Because it's afraid of a greater disorder.
The brain needs order in conformity because that's how the brain has been trained since childhood.

What'll happen if I live totally in the past, thinking that's the proper way to live?
When I've found an order, a belief, a hope, that I don't want questioned by anybody....
With this fear I propose another type of routine.
When we're neither seeking nor striving, the mind becomes extraordinarily alert, active, silent. It becomes part of a different dimension which thought can never reach. It's a spiritual state of mind.

Can consciousness be aware of what it's thinking?
Can thought understand its structure?
Is it thought that becomes aware of itself or is it something else?
Test it now. Notice how you think.
It seems to be stopping.
No, it's experiencing a radical change.
According to quantum theory. the object, when observed though a microscope, cannot remain still. yet when apart from the act of observation, it becomes different.
In the field of consciousness, it's perception that changes. It can last a second.. that's enough... don't demand more.
CULTURE

K wants to liberate humanity from the destructive conditioning surrounding thought obsessed by itself.

His detailed analyses of thought force us into a vicious circle.

Liberty means nothing to him, if it doesn't liberate us from that.

He insists so much that 'thought isn't good' that people become obsessed, think that it's bad to think and so don't think.

Shortly after his meetings with K. Shainberg abandoned psychiatry and dedicated himself to painting.

One thing that Shainberg suggested is true: the followers of **K** appeared to have abandoned their feelings, their enjoyment of life, their sexuality and happiness. **K** too seemed to have lost a lot of that, towards the end of his life. He certainly appeared to be less happy...

India, 1976. Indira Gandhi declared a state of emergency. A Censorship Committee was created. **K** considered it made no sense going there if he couldn't speak freely. He travelled to New Delhi only after receiving guarantees from **Pupul Jayakar** (an intimate friend of Indira Gandhi) that he could say what he wished. But the objective of the trip was to recruit young academics and professionals as teachers in his schools. Rajghat, the Rishi Valley, Brockwood Park, Ojai ... they all needed new people.

Look, Rajesh, the world is mad. We need people with vision who can see with objectivity and without fragmentation.

These places must be converted into centres of light. Do you understand?

1977. **Indira Gandhi** called a general election and was defeated. **K** had a sudden premonition in which he foresaw the future.

We still have much grief and violence before us.

1979. **Indira Gandhi** spent four days in prison which caused uprisings in many parts of India. When she got out she met with **K** again.

That year, Indira Gandhi triumphed in the elections, by an astounding majority, and was nominated prime minister of India for a second time. **K** returned to his country several times in the following years despite the danger that the spread of his ideas still entailed.

Ojai, 1980. Although **K** was filled with a renewed energy after his last tour, he still decided to pay attention to his health. Dr. Janker discovered he had a hernia and advised an operation. He also prescribed him a diet for his diabetes and diagnosed the beginning of cataracts in both eyes.

The court found in favour of **K** in the judgement against Rajagopal and **K** recovered Oak Grove and Arya Vihara.

New York, 1982. K again lectured on Psychoanalysis and God. Important psychiatrists and psychotherapists, directors and professors of Institutes of Psychology, and other health professionals present, appeared lost for words on hearing his ideas about unitary thought,

For **K** there was no difference between the observer and the observed, between the thinker and the thought, the one who had the experience and the experience itself. Psychoanalysis seemed to him to create as much dependence as religious dogma.

India, 1984

On the 31st October in New Delhi, Indira Gandhi was assassinated, shot dead by two of her security guards. K was deeply affected but he didn't abandon that year's tour. Pupul Jayakar accompanied him nearly all the time.

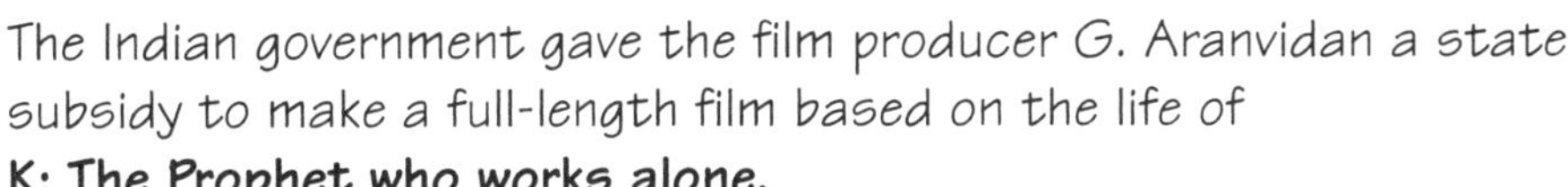

The Indian government gave the film producer G. Aranvidan a state subsidy to make a full-length film based on the life of
K: The Prophet who works alone.

We don't love the earth, we only exploit it. If we reject utilitarianism, we'll discover our tenderness and sensitivity once again.

'Be open, Pupul'... 'Be aware'... I'll do it immediately. I'll absorb..no, better still, I'll find out what I think and feel here and now. Oh, it's like going into a room and seeing everything in it at a glance.

Don't judge. don't condemn. clear the impurities from your mind so that you can see...

Walking by his side. one feels such a sense of silence. beauty and compassion. that it's difficult to ask him anything.

That's where the essence of his serenity dwells. He always appears to be beyond and yet be more in the here and now.

Every image is resistance. When the resistance no longer exists. then there'll be vulnerability but without the psychological wounds.

In Europe the publication of his book **The Ending of Time** awoke the interest of a new public. A professional film crew came to the Brockwood meeting in 1985 to make another film, **The Role of the Flower**. While the film was being shown on British television, **K** at 90 years of age continued travelling and speaking in search of people with clarity and vision.

USA. He participated in a symposium about Creativity in Science at the Centre of Atomic Research in Los Alamos. This provided him with a new and stimulating audience. He was also invited to speak at the Pacem in Terris Society , in the United Nations auditorium . The Austrian-American **Fritjof Capra** whose book **The Tao of Physics** was already a classic of the New Paradigm, heard him and was both fascinated and disturbed.

In Madras he told me to stop thinking, to liberate myself from knowledge and put reason to one side.

What should I do? Abandon my scientific career or abandon any hope... of spiritual self-realisation?

Capra felt rather intimidated, but in less than 10 seconds **K** had answered him:

After visiting him, Capra began to meditate regularly. His meeting with **K** was a changing point in his career.

In another conference, **K** maintained that desire originates in perception, that a sensory response follows this perception and then up comes thought with: 'I want this' or I don't want it'.

What **K** didn't say was: how to obtain this freedom. Like Buddha he posed the problem brilliantly, but unlike Buddha he didn't provide a clear path to freedom. Could it be that he hadn't liberated himself sufficiently from all conditioning so as to be able to lead his disciples towards complete self -realisation?

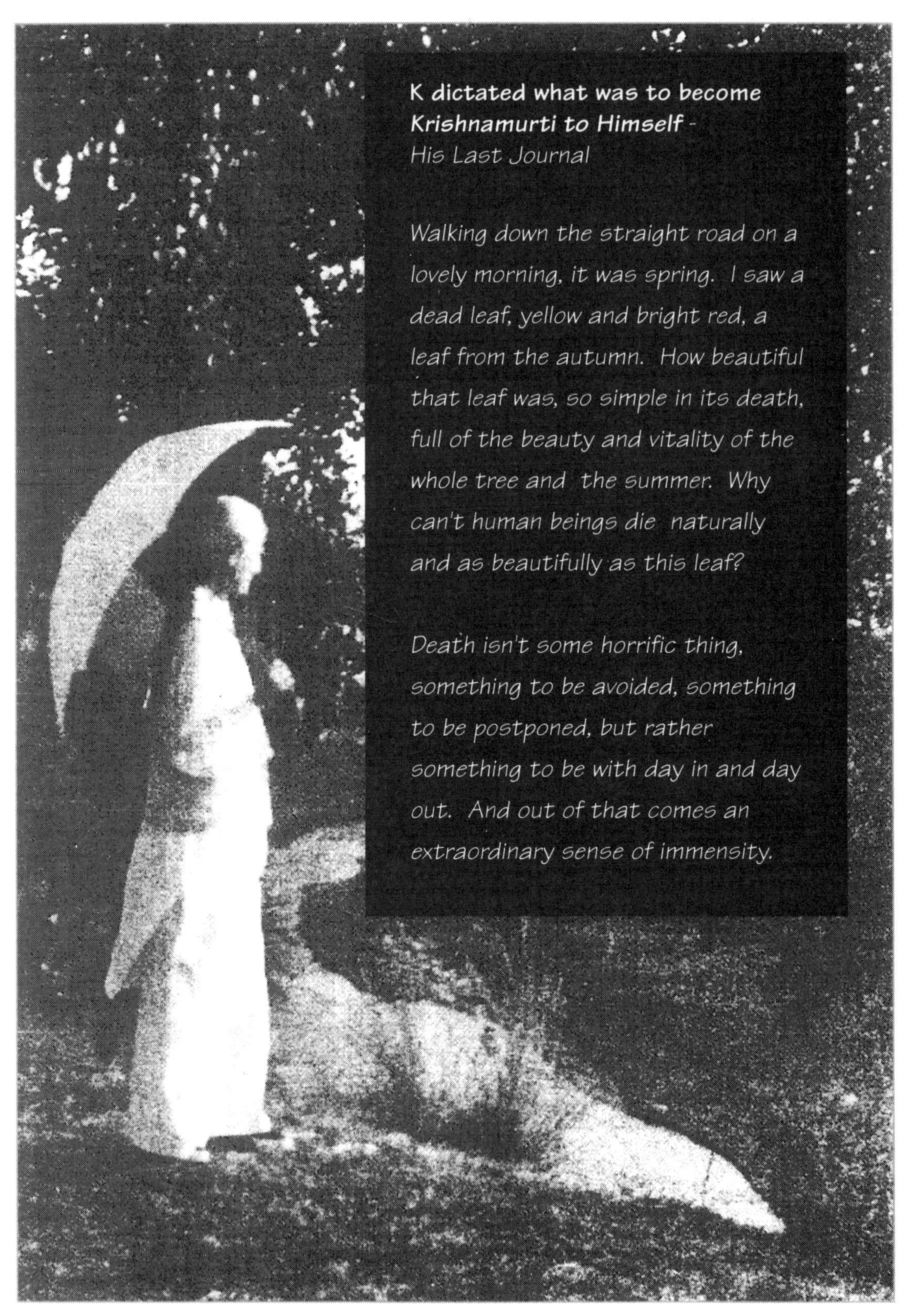
K dictated what was to become *Krishnamurti to Himself* -
His Last Journal
Walking down the straight road on a lovely morning, it was spring. I saw a dead leaf, yellow and bright red, a leaf from the autumn. How beautiful that leaf was, so simple in its death, full of the beauty and vitality of the whole tree and the summer. Why can't human beings die naturally and as beautifully as this leaf?
Death isn't some horrific thing, something to be avoided, something to be postponed, but rather something to be with day in and day out. And out of that comes an extraordinary sense of immensity.

VII Last steps in the 20th Century

Madras, 1986. Thousands of people waited in Vasan Vihar. **K** arrived on foot with his nephew Narayan.

In one hour **K**'s talk covered birth, the principles of all energy and the perception of the path leading to the spring of creation. Then he remained seated in silence. A boy brought him a white flower. He took it in his hands and smiled. The talk came to an end. People around him already knew that it would be his last appearance in public.

Asit Chandmal author of the book **The Last Walk** recounted that the following day **K** met his 18 year old daughter Clea and they talked at length about molecular biology, genetics and other sciences - and what would happen when they began to use computer technology. Before leaving, she told him she was going to study at Cambridge.

Weak, much thinner, **K** spent many hours a day in bed; but not for a single afternoon did he miss his walk ...

It was always the same walk by the sea, in Adyar. **K** went along the shoreline where he was 'discovered', adopted and initiated 75 years earlier. Nearby was the house of Radha Burnier, the current president of the Theosophical Society.

At 34 years old, when he left the Society and renounced everything they'd given him, **K** had already said the same thing. Now, in silence, he looked for the last time at that sea and that sky. At midnight, an aeroplane was to take him to the US.

Ojai

K was taken into hospital on arrival. A prestigious oncologist Dr. Deutsch confirmed he had cancer of the pancreas, which had spread to the liver. There was no possibility that he would recover. **K** didn't want to die in hospital. On the 30th January, they allowed him to return to Pine Cottage.

For seventy years.. that immense energy.. that immense intelligence ... has been using his body as a vehicle. Now it can take no more.

The same night four people flew from Delhi to Los Angeles bringing a silver urn with them.

K barely recognised them. He could only concentrate for a few seconds. His eyes closed.

On Wednesday February 12th, Halley's Comet, after circling the Sun, began to move away from it. **K** suffered a violent hemorrhage.

A violent storm hurled itself inland from the Pacific. For two days the roads to Ojai were lashed with unprecedented rain. Mud built up on the route running through the valley. It was feared that Pine Cottage would remain completely isolated. Some homes were evacuated, television units filmed the deluge in Ojai.

After the storm, Asit Chandmal spoke to **K**.

How can I help you? I don't mean your body, which is being cared for...

Don't let anyone spoil my teaching.

Later, when he found out that Asit was visiting Silicon Valley, **K** called him:

What's the latest news on computers? Is it true that the Russians are spying and that the Japanese are catching up with the others?

He listened to me so attentively that I thought I was conversing with the same old K.

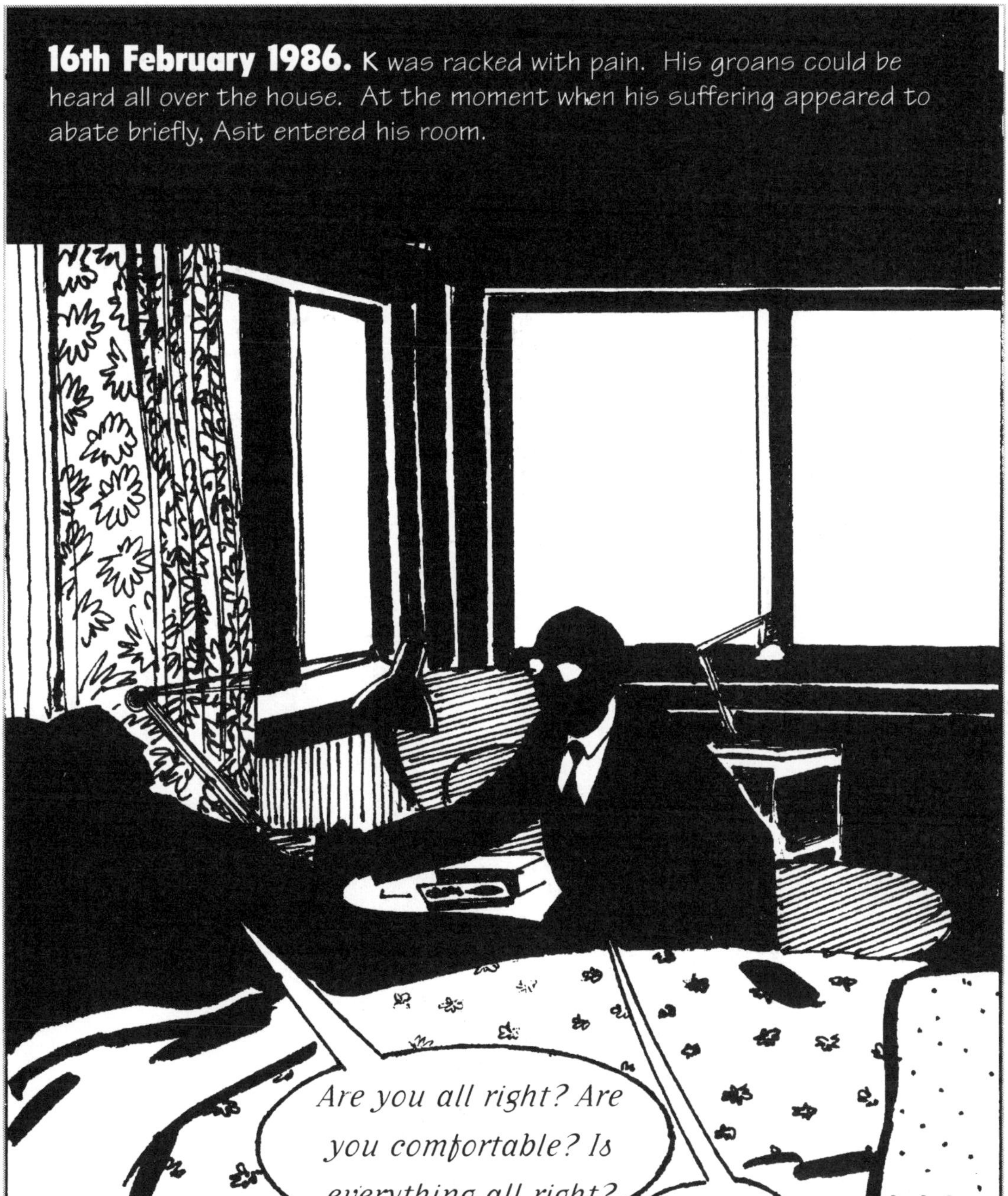

16th February 1986. K was racked with pain. His groans could be heard all over the house. At the moment when his suffering appeared to abate briefly, Asit entered his room.

Shortly after midnight, he died in his sleep.

The Indian Times

KRISHNAMURTI DIED

(*Asit Chandmal*) The pain began early in the morning. By noon he had required a substantial amount of medication by late in the afternoon K had drifted off intermittently into a sleep. When the pain was most intense, K seemed to be the most lucid. He stated he did not want to go on like this. I felt that he would not survive another day of pain and I was quite concerned about his suffering, as I had promised him he would feel no more pain. I was frustrated in that I wanted to be at his side, but I felt that I had neglected my family since I was spending so much time at K's bedside. But I felt that this was most likely Krishnamurti's last day with us. K quieted and his respiration seemed to slow down. I was amazed at how strong K was and I attributed this to his extremely well-kept body. At this point, I felt he was feeling no pain although his respiration and pulse were slowing. I sent Patrick, the r.N., to the kitchen to get Mary, as I knew that she would to be at his bedside at the very end. He stopped breathing at six minutes past midnight and his final pulse beat was detected at ten minutes after fifteen seconds in the early morning hours of February 17, 1986. I gently closed his eyes.a

The ashes were divided between three urns: one for the United States, another for England and the third, the silver one, returned to India.

New Delhi received the ashes of **Jiddu Krishnamurti** in a heavy hailstorm. The ground was momentarily covered with small white hailstones. Immediately afterwards the urn was surrounded by flowers. At that moment the sun came out again.

In his schools teaching continued along the lines of ' deconditioning'. People from around the world went to the Foundations to use their resources. Videos of his speeches and discussions became study material and were regularly shown on TV cultural channels. Major publishers continued to reprint his books in every language.
Disciples of truth
If K was surprised when no-one understood what he was saying. he would be even more surprised to see how much he's understood now.
Who are the people interpreting his message today? What validity do a man's words have when they were spoken 30, 40, 50 years ago? His words return time and time again to the same themes - fear, intelligence, suffering, awareness, etc. He may seem to be speaking at a high level of abstraction, but there are certain things that those who read, listen to or study him fully understand...

→ **...people know** that he never repeats himself, and that the important thing is their perception of what Krishnamurti is saying rather than its literal meaning. And **they know** that what he's talking about is how each of them deals with that perception, how they relate to it and integrate it into themselves without carving it in stone.

→ **... they know** that Truth is not found in dogma or formula, and that no teacher can replace the word of his own consciousness.

Truth is not contained by consciousness but is a channel leading towards it.

→ **... they know** that the stronger the tradition - family, cultural, social, religious - the more difficult it is for us to accept the mystery that each moment offers us.

→ **... they know** that many accepted truths are only projections of past experiences, the remains of previously thought ideas, hopes that disguise basic fears.

→ **... they know** that when educators don't put Truth in a closed box, but allow free expression...that when children can explore new paths without preconceptions and without fear....that when men and women try to clear their mind of memories, expectations, certainties... nothing else seems abstract. Everything takes on another meaning and the Truth will be silhouetted on the horizon.

Many who searched for the meaning of life on this planet, who expected to find in Krishnamurti the World Teacher, the Future Christ, and who followed him all their lives, realised - in time! - that he was not the Source, but that something Eternal was expressed 'through' him.
I have to tell you. K didn't have a mission
He had a teaching
Truth is engraved on the heart of every human being
When this is understood, there's no supreme revelation ... but there's a **profound liberation**

I never found it easy to do what Krishnamurti proposed: to live in a state of permanent awareness (free of conditioning, of the past, of fears,etc). Neither could I ever learn it like a lesson for the year and a half that I've been working on this book. I read hundreds of pages by K and about K and now and again I saw his videos. I dissected one after another of his speeches from different periods in search of a synthesis of his teaching. I allowed his message to penetrate that part of the mind where I don't believe I'm in control of anything, not even what I imagine. I followed his advice. I didn't convert myself into a disciple of any idea or person, not even of him. I tried not to deceive myself with the explanations I was obtaining - and translating into this book. Something 'stayed' with me from this relationship with his work: K helped me to break down the certainty I held, based on my knowledge about some things. At a level beyond words, where I have no control, I feel relief. It's as if the burden of supporting, feeding and maintaining the knowledge that shapes my personality had stopped being a tension conditioning my actions. Say whatever you like, Krishnamurti persuaded me to overcome the barrier of knowledge. Without being asked he helped to get rid of the basic fear in me created by the unknown. He taught me to give myself to what each situation dictates and to learn from it as a beginner. That 'being open to experience' is not the truth...it provides me with another link to it. Whether it exists or not, whether one has to search for it , whether it appears.. one never knows.. one should just be open and aware.

(the author)

Krishnamurti glossary

Action: action, in Krishnamurti's thought, is direct perception untrammelled by idealisation, comparison, judgement or memory. It is what one does 'when suddenly confronted by a tiger'.

Love: Love tied to circumstances and time is not true love. It's a state of union within which no space exists between the observer and the thing observed.

To learn and learning: K establishes a distinction between 'to learn', an accumulative process related to memory and thus to time, and another skill which he called 'learning' which is not an accumulative process and does not depend on time.

Beauty: The state of beauty is ' total action that operates when inaction is total'.

Self-knowledge: It is vital movement, a self- consciousness, an awareness of what is happening at each moment

Right thinking and right thought: These two terms describe contradictory things. Right thinking would be to think precisely, with a depth of understanding and lucidity. Right thought would be the habitual process of memory, judgement, comparison and the I.

Discipline: For him, this word has nothing to do with imitation, conformity, oppression, repression, adaptability or fear. It is tied to learning. We are incapable of learning without discipline " There is a major difference between disciplining oneself and being disciplined by others."

Religious spirit: The religious spirit as conceived by **K** has nothing to do with dogmas, rituals or spiritual or religious organisations. It's the spirit which is in a perpetual state of resurrection - or, to explain it better, that constantly dies for the past - . When man concentrates on the past, incapable of living this resurrection moment by moment, he is always projecting a hypothetical future, damaging religion and casting it in stone.

Mind: At first, this word meant to him at the same time, thought, will, emotion: years later he appears to have excluded pure perception from the concept of mind. He ended by defining the term by adding the word 'heart'; so he used mind-heart to clarify that he was also talking about the emotions.

Negative thought and positive thought. The rigid process of positive thought, maintained through accumulation, suffocates man. Negative thought with its constant questioning is a state of mental awareness that leads to the destruction of positive thought and an awareness of interior silence. Only this last state, which is not something thought about but something alive, can lead to the truth.

To break through: It means breaking the psychic chains which imprison consciousness to discover reality.

Uniqueness: It's the state of the individual who no longer identifies with the external world, because he has discovered so much of what makes his own individuality and character completely human.

Background: These are the elements of the past that condition the state of awareness and what we identify with. The Self formed in this way is a filter through which consciousness sees a deformed reality.

Selected bibliography

Mary Lutyens, **Krishnamurti - The Years of Awakening**, John Murray 1975

Krishnamurti's Journal, Victor Gollanz, 1982

Krishnamurti (with Dr David Bohm) , **The Ending of Time,** 1985

Pupul Jayakar, **Krishnamurti: a biography**, Harper & Row, 1986

Krishnamurti To Himself - His Last Journal, Victor Gollanz, 1987

Mary Lutyens, **The Life and Death of Krishnamurti**, John Murray, 1990

Juan Carlos Kreimer is an Argentinian writer. Among other books he has published **Punk, the young death** (1977), **To be as we are** (1988), **How should I write it?** (1989), **The sacred boy** (1991). He is the editor of the Beginners series in Spanish.

Martin Arvallo is an Argentinian illustrator. He worked in animated film. He is the graphics editor of the magazine Comic Guyana. He collaborated with the newspaper Renacer. He Illustrated the novel ' The divine button'. He studies violin. He also illustrated **Castaneda for Beginners.™**

index

M

N

O

P

Q

R

S

T

U

V

W

Z